A HISTORY OF SPARTA

950–192 B.C.

A HISTORY OF SPARTA

950–192 B.C.

W. G. Forrest

Fellow of Wadham College, Oxford, and
University Lecturer in Ancient History

W · W · NORTON & COMPANY

New York · London

Books That Live
The Norton imprint on a book means that in the publisher's
estimation it is a book not for a single season but for the years.
W. W. Norton & Company, Inc.

W. W. Norton & Company, Inc., 500 Fifth Avenue, New York, N.Y. 10110
W. W. Norton & Company Ltd., 37 Great Russell Street, London WC1B 3NU

SBN 393 00481-3

To Maurice Bowra
for his seventieth birthday

CONTENTS

FOREWORD

In so short a work it is impossible to give detailed references for everything. Rather than be selective I have omitted footnotes altogether but have tried at the end of each chapter to mention a few books and articles which will best introduce the reader to the evidence, the issues and earlier works on the subject. If I have preferred to list works in English it is not always because I think them better than those in other languages.

Many friends have helped me generously; I can name only a few, T. C. W. Stinton, N. D. Worswick, Professors A. Andrewes, G. Devereux and G. Huxley, but I am grateful to all of them. Above all I should like to thank Professor H. T. Wade-Gery, who has read the whole text, re-read, made me re-think and, I hope, improve much of it.

ABBREVIATIONS

BSA: Annual of the British School at Athens

CQ: Classical Quarterly

JHS: Journal of Hellenic Studies

CAH: Cambridge Ancient History

AJA: American Journal of Archaeology

CP: Classical Philology

Rev. Ét. Grècques: Revue des Études Grècques

Proc. Afr. Class. Ass: Proceedings of the African Classical Association

RIL: Rendiconti dell' Istituto Lombardo

Rh. Mus: Rheinisches Museum

CR: Classical Review

FGH: Fragmente der Griechischen Historiker

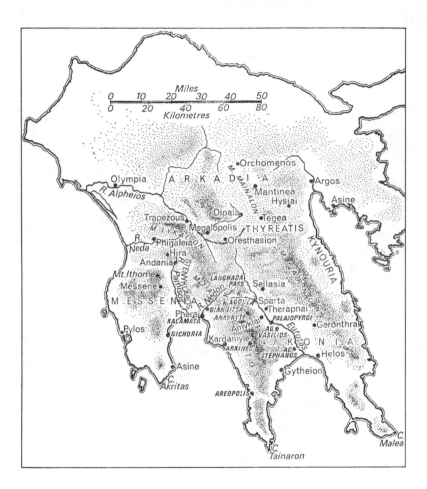

I

THE SOURCES

The southern Peloponnese, like so much of Greece, is a complex of mountains and valleys. In the east the once thickly wooded range of Parnon, running south to Cape Malea, leaves only tiny pockets of cultivable ground facing the Aegean; in the west a wider and softer coastal plain is bounded by a less continuous but still in parts formidable range formed by Mounts Lykaion, Ithome and the hills of Cape Akritas; down the centre, from the borders of Arkadia in the north to the tip of Cape Tainaron, the cliffs and gullies of Mount Taygetos make an almost unbroken barrier between east and west. Thus there are two main areas of cultivation and civilisation; one, at the head of the deep gulf between Akritas and Tainaron, was Messenia, the rich, utterly flat, alluvial plain of the Pamisos and its tributaries; the other behind the parallel gulf sheltered by Tainaron and Malea, the valley of the Eurotas, Laconia.

The Eurotas finds its way to the sea across a wide marshy plain which it enters through a limestone ridge connecting Parnon with Taygetos. North of the ridge is Laconia's central plain, some twenty miles long, some seven miles wide, well watered and fertile but more broken than its Messenian counterpart by small hills and ridges and, except to the west where Taygetos rises sheer above it, less well defined; to the south the ridge makes an effective psychological but no great physical barrier between it and the sea, eastwards rolling hills lead up to the heights of Parnon, to the north the valley narrows and rises erratically for some way before the Eurotas is lost in the foothills of the Arkadian mountains. Messenia is altogether a more open country. The Pamisos, rising in Mount Lykaion, flows at first through a fairly narrow gap firmly bounded by Ithome and the northern spurs of Taygetos, but this opens directly into a wide, flat, coastal plain, while both north and south of Ithome there are broad upland openings to the western sea.

Two distinct units, then, Laconia and Messenia, and communications between them were far from easy. The main mass of Taygetos which overlaps the Spartan plain to north and south can be crossed at several points and although it seems unlikely that the modern route from Sparta to Kalamata, the Langhada pass, was used in antiquity, there are traces which suggest communication a little to the south, through Arkines to Kardamyle and perhaps through Anavryte to Giannitsa. But neither could have offered an easy carriage road, even in summer. Much less tough though much longer was the pass which is followed by the modern road across Tainaron from Gytheion to Areopolis, but it gives access to no very open coastal route northwards into Messenia proper. Much less tough too, but exposed to Arkadian interference from the north, was a road up the Eurotas valley, around the northernmost spur of Taygetos (skirting the Arkadian plain of Megalopolis) and so down into the head of the Pamisos valley. Otherwise there was nothing but mountain tracks or the dangerous sea passage from gulf to gulf around stormy Tainaron.

Yet, for all this natural separation, the greater part of Laconia and Messenia was controlled for nearly 350 years (from about 715 to 370 B.C., the years which concern us most) by one city of the Laconian plain, Sparta. It is only with the annexation of Messenia that any Spartans become, for us, men of flesh and blood and that something like a continuous account of Spartan history becomes possible; with the loss of Messenia after 370 Sparta began the long decline that turned her by the beginning of our era into nothing more than an unpleasant memorial to all that had been most detestable in her past.

What is known of the decline we shall examine later; at the steps by which she became a power in Laconia itself and then crossed Taygetos into Messenia we can only guess. The tradition is rich enough in stories and in theories, fantastic and plausible, wild and sober, but for these early centuries stories are not true just because they are plausible nor are theories correct because they are sober—or even because they fit the facts. The facts are too few. To give the stories credit or the theories substance archaeology is needed but neither Laconia nor Messenia has as yet been more than scratched by the archaeologist.

There has been an excellent survey of prehistoric sites, complete for Laconia, partial for Messenia, and this has been reinforced by excavation at the Mycenaean palace of Nestor at Pylos, at Agios Stephanos in South Laconia, at Amyklai and Therapnai in the Spartan plain. But for the period after the collapse of the Mycenaean kingdoms there has been no thorough survey and virtually no excavation outside Sparta itself; while even in Sparta only one or two areas have been systematically explored—the sanctuary of Artemis Orthia and the Akropolis, for example. Thus there is no archaeological picture of Laconia during the period of Sparta's expansion in it or of Messenia before its annexation; nothing to show the effects of Sparta's domination on either, and only a few glimpses of the Messenia recreated after 370 and of the new Laconia of the Roman conquest. The little we have from Sparta itself is good: the excavations, early though they were, were conducted thoroughly and intelligently, but in using their evidence it must always be remembered that they were limited. The finds from the Orthia sanctuary disprove beyond doubt the traditional picture of an austere and gloomy sixth-century Sparta but they do not justify some of the sweeping positive assertions that have been based on them.

In some cases the need for archaeological information can be exaggerated; George Grote's picture of fifth-century Athens, drawn more than a century ago, is largely true and would still be true if we found a million more pots and another Parthenon, this because the Greeks themselves knew pretty well what Athens was like. But about Sparta they knew little and what they knew was seen by way of so many distorting mirrors that the modern historian cannot easily arrive at the original reflection, this in spite of the fact that Sparta for long was (and to many for longer seemed) the most important state in Greece.

It is easy to list the reasons for distortion. For one thing, no native of Sparta before Sosibios in the late third century B.C. chose to share his knowledge systematically with the outside world. In the seventh century the poet Tyrtaios, who must have played a significant part in the Messenian war of his time and the political upheavals that went with it, wrote propaganda poems to urge his fellow Spartans on in battle and calm them down in politics—the few fragments which survive are the most important evidence we have for the Spartan revolution; a generation later Alkman produced a series of charming lyrics for Spartan choirs to sing at festivals—again the fragments add a much-needed dimension of gaiety and colour to what we think of early Sparta; about 400 B.C. the king Pausanias wrote a tendentious pamphlet on the laws of Lykourgos—though it is lost, later Greeks may have learnt from it. But a few lines from 'Over There', 'Smoke Gets in your Eyes' and a speech by President Johnson on America's Far Eastern policy would make a poor basis for a history of twentieth-century America. And even Sosibios when he came was a Hellenistic antiquarian, not a political historian—again surviving only in fragments.

From time to time an interested foreigner was welcomed—Herodotos in the mid-fifth century was told tales of what his host's grandfather had done in the Samian war, heard bits of scandal about the royal houses, even a few remarks on the constitution and its history, but a Thucydides who asked professional questions about the Spartan army met with suspicion, hostility and silence—'I could not find out because of their secretiveness'.

But far more damaging than the restricted range of a foreigner's view were the prejudices which came to colour what he saw. Already by the late fifth century Sparta had become the paragon of Greek oligarchies as Athens was the model for democracies. Hellanikos of Lesbos, democratically inclined, may have refused to admit that Sparta's constitution had given her centuries of untroubled peace; on the other hand the aristocrat Herodotos and the oligarchic sympathiser Thucydides, clear-sighted critics though they were, perhaps exaggerated that peace. Spartan history and Spartan society were becoming issues in political and philosophical debate. Much worse was to come.

In 404 B.C. Athens lost the Peloponnesian War. An extraordinary experiment in imperialism had failed and the bright world she had built to dazzle the whole of Greece for fifty years collapsed. Foreigners might rejoice or lament according to taste but for Athenians the shock went deeper. Even the most extreme of her oligarchs had grown up to take Athenian greatness for granted, to share the pride which Athenians felt in their city and what it had done, even secretly to admire the democracy that had made it possible. How could lumbering antique Sparta have defeated Athens, their Athens? Plato, Xenophon and Isokrates were all young men in 404; they all asked themselves the question, and their answers affected the rest of their lives. Isokrates, the shallow rhetorician, was less troubled than the others—he took refuge in sentimental dreams about the days when Athens and Sparta had fought together against the Persians and, from time to time, saw an unreal contemporary Sparta as a possible leader in a new crusade; the soldier Xenophon turned to hero-worship of the contemporary Spartan military machine and its military leaders, perfect products of a perfect and unchanging system; the moralist Plato was able to persuade himself that something like the austerity, the discipline, above all the authoritarianism of Sparta could help ordinary men towards, indeed was necessary if ordinary men were ever to reach, the 'good life'. Together with other members of their generation they built up a mythical Sparta, contemporary and historical, from which later Greeks could never quite escape.

When Sparta in turn met disaster at Leuktra in 371 it became a little easier to see her as she really was. At the same time there was new evidence to hand, for fourth-century scholars were the first to realise that poetry and documents should be searched systematically for historical information—Tyrtaios had been known as a martial poet, now he became a historical source, and it is probable that the *Rhetra* too, the most important document we have on early Spartan history, was first sought out and studied in the mid-fourth century. Thus Aristotle's account of the Spartan constitution, the *Lakedaimonion Politeia*, written perhaps about 330, is the one ancient work on the subject whose loss is most regrettable. Aristotle's political insight applied to the evidence then available could not but have produced a real basis for understanding—though no doubt it would be read with the same ungrateful grumblings that have greeted his comparable account of Athens. Even so the few surviving fragments of the *Politeia* together with stray remarks in the *Politics* show that he too had to waste much energy in debunking the myth that would have been better spent establishing the truth, and often enough even he fails to see that myth was myth.

No one afterwards had his genius or his opportunity. Already in the fifth century Greeks acquired the idea that a balance between different elements in a state would ensure stability and peace. It was a short step from there to the belief that Sparta's model stability rested on this principle of balance—her kings were the monarchic element, her

Gerousia the aristocratic, her assembly the democratic (one scholar added
the ephors as oligarchic)—and the doctrine, worked out in the course
of the fourth century, became a commonplace among hellenistic political
theorists. One substantial version, which survives reapplied to Rome in
the sixth book of Polybios, shows just how firmly the developed myth
was established by the second century B.C. For although Polybios hated
his contemporary Sparta and was not a man to hide his prejudices, he
does not deny this totally false image of Sparta's past; he can only
claim that contemporary Sparta had betrayed its heritage.

So indeed it had, if not as Polybios thought. The idea of survival, of
stability, was central to all admiration of Sparta, though oligarchs,
philosophers and political theorists between them had concocted an
unreal vision of what had survived. Change was therefore unthinkable. And so, when third-century Spartan politicians decided that
change was needed, they began by turning the story upside down—they
were recreating what had once been stable and perfect. Somehow the
myth had to be tailored to match their aims—and both the myth and
their aims suffered as a result. The philosopher Sphairos acted as adviser
to the reforming king, Kleomenes III—how much was his advice
coloured by what he genuinely knew about 'Lykourgan' Sparta, how
far was his picture of 'Lykourgan' Sparta corrupted by the temptation
to apply his own philosophical ideas in practice? The influential general
historian of the third century, Phylarchos, so admired the ideals of
Kleomenes that he centred his whole story around Sparta—his fragments and Polybios' comments on them show that his bias affected his
story of the present; presumably it also affected any implications the
story it may have had for the past.

The politically important part of the reformers' work was soon un-
done though much was left untouched, deliberately or inadvertently.
But how much of what was then restored was 'genuine', whatever that
now means, is just as unclear as how much of the reformers' own work
had been restoration or innovation. Another barrier between us and
early Sparta. There was one more to come. The Roman conquerors of
Greece found much that was congenial in the ideas of 'Lykourgos',
and, with the principate, began to indulge a frivolous antiquarianism
by turning such relics as they found into a tourist attraction. 'Crowds
flock from all sides . . . to watch the spectacle [of boys being flogged
at the altar of Artemis Orthia] and they watch it with pleasure and

enthusiasm.' So wrote Philostratos in the third century A.D. It is hard to believe that the Spartans they flocked to see were any more like their ancestors, even their third-century B.C. ancestors, than the modern Sioux in his reserve is like the man who destroyed Custer or the Huns of Cinecitta like the men who followed Attila.

Yet this was the Sparta that gave life to the most extensive writings on Spartan history we have, the biographies of Plutarch, who in the early second century A.D. tried to make coherent sense out of the mass of tradition and counter-tradition, theory and counter-theory that now surrounded the museum; this was the Sparta whose antiquities the traveller Pausanias, a little later, tried to describe.

There are two further sources of confusion. The new Messenia established by the Thebans after Leuktra had to have a history. But although four centuries of slavery or a century or more of exile will not blot out entirely a people's recollection of their past, they do not encourage completeness or accuracy and there is no denying that, faced with gaps and contradictions, historians were prepared to theorise or to romance their way to a detailed story. Kallisthenes of Olynthos (about 340 B.C.) was one of the first to exploit Tyrtaios as a historical source, possibly the first to use what he found there as the foundation for a highly imaginative and largely fantastic saga of heroic Messenian resistance to the Spartans; first but by no means the last, and the quality of Spartan history was not improved by the contamination.

Finally there is the question of chronology. An early Greek dated the past by generations. To answer the question 'How long ago?' fifth-century scholars then gave a fixed length to a generation, thus allowing a rough answer and at the same time a crude correlation between the private family traditions of different states. At the centre of the 'system' they put the lists of the two Spartan royal houses; naturally enough—they were the most significant and, going back as they did to Herakles, must have been among the longest. But to make them match, even with each other, some surgery would be needed and, in the upper reaches of the Eurypontid line, there are signs that surgery may have been applied. And neither clarity nor correlation was improved by the fact that scholars disagreed on a generation's length, some positing forty, some roughly thirty, years.

A little later more accurate and more reliable methods were devised —by about 400 lists had been published of Olympic victors (by

Hippias of Elis), of victors at the Spartan Karneia (by Hellanikos of Lesbos), of Athenian archons (by the state), and although a few of the entries in the victor lists may have been due to scholarly guesswork rather than solid evidence, it is absurd to doubt their overall reliability. Many Greeks, however, were not impressed; only a restricted number of events could be securely tied to a victor or even to an archon and, more important, the lists themselves covered only a part of the past (the longest, from Olympia, went back to 776). The lists were accepted but for the vital centuries before 776, the legendary centuries with which most Greek scholars were primarily concerned, generations remained the only tool. There had to be a reconciliation and again the Spartan kings, and with them Spartan history, were at the heart of the struggle. During it Sparta too was given an annual list, eponymous ephors going back to 754 (below p 76 f.), but that did not help; in its higher levels it is almost certainly pure invention, and, in consequence, no events were attached to the names that figured on it.

Charon of Lampsakos (*c.* 400) may have tried to match kings with ephors, Timaios of Tauromenion (*c.* 300), who may have concocted the ephor-list, matched kings, ephors and other lists as well, Eratosthenes (*c.* 230) and his follower Apollodoros (*c.* 150) produced a general table which became the standard chronicle of antiquity. None of these was a fool or a rogue but they had an almost impossible task and to us, who can rarely be sure of what they wrote and hardly ever of how they arrived at it, there are no more than half a dozen rock-hard dates before 650 and few enough thereafter.

There is need for caution, then, but not for despair. The date of the first Messenian War (*c.* 735–715) is indirectly based on Olympic records and even more indirectly and hesitantly supported by archaeology; we know the name of the Spartan king who won it, Theopompos. The date of Sparta's defeat by Argos at Hysiai (669) is derived from an Olympic date and we can be fairly sure of the name of the Spartan king who lost it, Polydoros. There are firm if sometimes approximate dates for all the kings from about 520 onwards and almost firm dates for two generations before that. Given all this and the certainty that generations do average about thirty years, a chronological map can be drawn back to about 800, a map on which the lines are blurred but are none the less certain—so long as we leave them blurred. I set out the map below, adding for completeness the area before 800 which must still be marked 'unexplored'.

AGIADS		EURYPONTIDS	
Agis I	[930–900]	Eurypon	[895–865]
Echestratos	[900–870]	Prytanis	[865–835]
Leobotas	[870–840]	Polydektes	[835–805]
Dorussos	[840–815]	Eunomos	[805–775]
Agesilaos I	[815–785]	Charillos	c. 775–750
Archelaos	c. 785–760	Nikandros	c. 750–720
Teleklos	c. 760–740	Theopompos	c. 720–675
Alkamenes	c. 740–700	Anaxandridas I	c. 675–660
Polydoros	c. 700–665	Archidamos I	c. 660–645
Eurykrates	c. 665–640	Anaxilas	c. 645–625
Anaxandros	c. 640–615	Leotychidas I	c. 625–600
Eurykratidas	c. 615–590	Hippokratidas	c. 600–575
Leon	c. 590–560	Agasikles	c. 575–550
Anaxandridas II	c. 560–520	Ariston	c. 550–515
Kleomenes I	c. 520–490	Demaratos	c. 515–491

It is hard to accept the Spartan claim that son had succeeded father without exception up to this point and I have therefore arbitrarily reduced some of the earlier figures to allow for an occasional succession in the same generation; later irregularities stem from historical arguments of varying force (Teleklos, for example, is given twenty, Alkamenes forty years, because the former is said to have been assassinated). After 490 the succession is more complicated and I indicate the relationship of each king to his predecessor in brackets.

Leonidas I	490–480	Leotychidas II	491–469
(brother)		(distant cousin—greatgrandson of	
Pleistarchos	480–459	Hippokratidas)	
(son)		Archidamos II	469–427
Pleistoanax	459–409	(grandson)	
(cousin)		Agis II	427–399
Pausanias	409–395	(son)	
(son)		Agesilaos II	399–360
Agesipolis I (son)	395–380	(brother)	
Kleombrotos I	380–371	Archidamos III	360–338
(brother)		(son)	

Agesipolis II (son)	371–370	Agis III (son)	338–331
Kleomenes II (brother)	370–309	Eudamidas I (brother)	c. 331–305
Areus I (grandson)	309–265	Archidamos IV (son)	c. 305–275
Akrotatos (son)	265–c. 262	Eudamidas II (son)	c. 275–244
Areus II (son)	c. 262–254	Agis IV (son)	c. 244–241
Leonidas II (grandson of Kleomenes II)	c. 254–236	Eudamidas III (son)	c. 241–228
Kleomenes III (son; in exile 222–219)	236–222	Archidamos V (uncle)	228–227
Agesipolis III (grandson of Kleombrotos II who ruled briefly during the exile of Leonidas II, 243–241)	219–215	Eukleidas (Agiad—brother of Kleomenes III)	227–222

There is much vagueness about the higher reaches of each list and some uncertainty—for greater symmetry some scholars introduced another Eurypontid, Soos, before the eponymous Eurypon; for no clear reason Pausanias gives quite different names for the four successors of Theopompos from those of Herodotos which are reproduced here and although he is wrong the doubt is disturbing. But the whole does provide a broadly safe framework to build on.

And as with chronology, so with history. Plutarch digested his sources, he did not simply repeat them, but it is often possible to see the inspiration of this or that sentiment (his lives of Agis IV and Kleomenes III, for example, are largely derived from Phylarchos), and usually safe to assume that he has not been stupid in his choice of information, for he was a highly intelligent man. Pausanias had less discrimination but he was an honest reporter of what he saw and a careful enough copier of what he read; the brief account he gives of Spartan history as an introduction to his tour of the surviving monuments is patchy but not despicable. We know something of the distortions, the many and serious distortions, which affected them and their sources, and allowances can be made. Consequently, so long as it is remembered that almost all their evidence, and all our other evidence, may be telling us about two entirely different things, about Sparta's past and about the then current state of the myth on Sparta's past, it is not entirely futile to think that some truth about that past can be discovered.

BIBLIOGRAPHY

Geography: A. Philippson and E. Kirsten, *Die Griechische Landschaften* III 371 ff. (with bibliography).

Archaeology: R. Hope-Simpson, *BSA 52* (1957) 231 ff.; Hope-Simpson and E. Waterhouse, *BSA 55* (1960) 67 ff. and *56* (1961) 114 ff. (general surveys); R. M. Dawkins, H. J. W. Tillyard, M. N. Tod, A. J. B. Wace, A. M. Woodward and others in *BSA 12–16* (1905/6–1909/10) and *26–30* (1923/4–1929/30) *passim* (excavations at Sparta and explorations elsewhere); R. M. Dawkins, *The sanctuary of Artemis Orthia* (1929); N. Valmin, *Études topographiques sur la Messénie ancienne* (1930).

The tradition: F. Ollier, *Le Mirage Spartiate* 2 vols. (Paris 1933 and 1943); E. N. Tigerstedt, *The Legend of Sparta* I (Lund 1965). For the various fragmentary authors mentioned see the text and commentary in F. Jacoby, *Die Fragmente der Griechischen Historiker*; see also L. Pearson, *Historia 11* (1962) 397 ff. (on the Messenian tradition), A. W. Gomme, *Historical Commentary on Thucydides* I 54 ff. (briefly on Plutarch as a historian), W. G. Forrest, *The Phoenix 17* (1963) 176 ff. (more briefly on Pausanias).

Chronology: A. R. Burn, *JHS 55* (1935) 130 ff. (cf. *JHS 69* (1949) 70); W. Den Boer, *Laconian Studies* part I; *Historia 5* (1956) 162 ff.; T. J. Dunbabin, *The Western Greeks* (Oxford, 1948) App. I; Forrest, art. cit. 166 ff.

2

THE ARRIVAL OF THE DORIANS

The early history of Laconia, as told by later Greeks, was fairly simple. By the time of the Trojan War, they said, the Eurotas valley was united in one powerful kingdom, its capital at or near the site of classical Sparta. This was Lakedaimon. Its king, Menelaos, husband of Helen, was the brother of Agamemnon who from Mykenai ruled the north-eastern Peloponnese and was in some vague way overlord of most of the other Greek principalities. Unlike many of the heroes who fought at Troy Menelaos returned safely to his kingdom which passed on his death to his nephew and son-in-law, Orestes; in turn to his grandson, Teisamenos. But then came catastrophe. A Greek tribe, the Dorians, who had previously lived in northern Greece on the edge of the civilised world, crossed the Korinthian Gulf and overran the great cities of the Peloponnese, Pylos in the south-west, Lakedaimon and Mykenai itself. The invaders were led by a family of exiled princes, descendants of Herakles, the two brothers, Kresphontes and Temenos, and the twin sons of a third brother, Eurysthenes and Prokles, and the greater part of the Peloponnese was divided among the three groups; the north-east went to Temenos, Messenia to Kresphontes, Laconia to Eurysthenes and Prokles. And so the pattern of the classical Peloponnese was established.

Different sources offer variants of detail (in some accounts the twins' father, Aristodemos, was still alive to lead the invasion) but the outline is firm; equally firm, though equally obscure in detail, is the story told by archaeology. During the thirteenth century B.C., roughly the archaeological period Late-Helladic III B, Laconia flourished; there were at least four substantial settlements in the Spartan plain, at Therapnai, at Amyklai (a sanctuary), at Palaiopyrgi and Agios Vasilios (probably the ancient Pharis and Bryseai respectively), and as many more in the southern coastal plain. All but one, Amyklai, appear to have been destroyed or abandoned at or soon after the end of Late-Helladic III B, i.e. about 1200, and except in Amyklai and on the eastern side of Parnon which belonged to the Aegean rather than to the mainland, Late-Helladic III C pottery has been found only in insignificant amounts on a handful of sites. Around 1200, then, Laconian civilisation, like that of so many other Mycenaean centres, was virtually obliterated.

Almost more striking is the fact that the invaders have left no mark of themselves. Scattered around the Spartan plain there was a sufficient population to maintain one centre, at Amyklai; a few other men left their pots around on sites near the southern coast, but these were survivors of the old régime, not the victorious carriers of a new culture or even of a new barbarism. It is two centuries or more before a new style of pottery begins to appear, the so-called proto-geometric, at Amyklai again, at the site of a new town, classical Sparta, and at places around the coast.

Either, then, a few invaders stayed behind to mingle with the survivors, to multiply and at last to develop a new culture; or at some time around 1000 there was a second wave of invasion, which brought with it or soon produced the earliest form of classical Spartan civilisation. As things stand archaeology does not rule out the first possibility but inclines towards the second.

The pattern of thirteenth-century settlement reflects well enough the kingdom of Menelaos as Homer describes it in a passage that goes back to a Mycenaean source. Of the identifiable cities which he mentions only Sparta itself has certainly failed to produce evidence of a Mycenaean community (this may be due to chance of excavation or to the transfer of the name of Menelaos' capital, wherever it was, to the later mistress of Laconia). Further, although the date of the sack of Troy is still disputed (opinion varies between c. 1260 and c. 1200), the destruction of this Laconian culture could well have fallen in the lifetime of the grandson of one of Troy's captors. Even some of the stories about refugees from the destruction find archaeological support—both in Kypros and on the north coast of the Peloponnese (the later Achaia) where traditions send fugitives from Laconia, there were newcomers in Late-Helladic III C.

Thus far, it seems, the Greeks may have remembered well, but there was certainly no Dorian settlement in Sparta or anywhere else in Laconia in Teisamenos' generation, nor for six generations or so thereafter. No Dorian warrior-élite crushed an earlier population and established at one blow a Dorian Sparta as mistress of an enslaved Laconia. The invaders of 1200, or the vast majority of them, moved on. The settlers of 1000 may also have been a warrior-élite, but if so they could not have practised their trade—their few potential opponents were in no state to offer much resistance, nor do the earliest remains from Sparta suggest much power or organisation. Dorians, of course, many of them must have been—it was their dialect and their tradition which later Spartans used—and the story later told of the destroyers could be broadly true of the settlers, an early home in northern Thessaly, a complicated itinerary through north-central Greece. There are traces on the ground which suggest some newcomers' progress through western Attika, the Argolid which they reached about 1050 and so into the southern Peloponnese. But whether the traces represent one more or less direct and simple move southwards or a random combination of drift and counter-drift in the comparative vacuum of post-Mycenaean Greece, we cannot say.

Just as uncertain are the nature and the extent of their contribution to the new culture of Laconia. The basic inspiration of proto-geometric came from Attika and it may have been the intruders who brought some awareness of Attic proto-geometric south with them. But the style which developed in Laconia was highly individual and it would seem to have grown up in Amyklai as well as in Sparta—Amyklai which had survived the invasion of 1200. This survival supports the tradition that there was no Dorian takeover there, though there may have been, of course, some Dorian infiltration or influence. And that is the core of the problem—should we think of a general take-over or of infiltration; if of take-over, by one or more than one group of newcomers (Herodotos records the admission of one non-Dorian element, 'Minyans' from Lemnos, into the Spartan community); if of infiltration by new into old, Dorians into Amyklai, or old into new, scattered pre-Dorians into, say, Sparta? In the end the Dorian language and the

Dorian mystique proved predominant, but how strong it was at the start, how much it contributed and how much it received, is hard to say. The ways of cultural, social and even of linguistic influence are too unpredictable.

By about 1000 B.C., however, the chief elements of Dorian Sparta were assembled in Laconia and the first steps were being taken towards its creation. At this point the Greek tradition again begins to make sense. Spartans traced the ancestry of their kings back through the eponymous founders of the two royal houses, Agis and Eurypon, to their fathers, Eurysthenes and Prokles, to Aristodemos and ultimately to Herakles. It was assumed that kings reigned for forty years and so, accidentally, roughly the right date was reached for the invaders, for the collapse of the Mycenaean kingdom. But a more realistic calculation gives not 1200 but 960–930 for Eurysthenes and Prokles, and 930–900 or thereabouts for Agis and Eurypon who as eponyms must be the real founders of their dynasties. Given that even a realistic calculation in these terms cannot be exact, that the current dating of the earliest Laconian proto-geometric pottery to 1000–950 B.C. is by no means firm, that there need not be an exact coincidence of initial settlement with the installation of either dynasty, there is here a comforting measure of agreement between archaeology and tradition.

In other words, later Greeks had a clear enough picture of the Mycenaean world; they also had a coherent story of the society which grew up on the ruins of that world but they had lost completely the measure of the dark years that came between. Mycenaean Lakedaimon vanished around 1200, Dorian Sparta was created somewhere in the tenth century (perhaps later rather than earlier for in this context genealogies may be more reliable than pots). Of what happened in between we have no knowledge.

BIBLIOGRAPHY

The archaeological background: V. d'A. Desborough, *The Last Mycenaeans and their Successors* (1964) ch. III. 3; cf. also F. Kiechle, *Lakonien und Sparta* (1963) ch. I. *The tradition:* H. T. Wade–Gery, *CAH* II 525 ff. and *AJA* (1948) 107 ff.; N. G. L. Hammond, *BSA 32* (1931/2) 131 ff. and *CAH* II 2nd ed. ch. 36.

3

THE CONQUEST OF LACONIA

The Sparta which was founded in the tenth century was not a city like those of the rest of Greece; 'if Sparta was deserted', wrote Thucydides, 'and only its temples and its ground plan left, future generations would never believe that its power had matched its reputation . . . without any urban unity, made up as it is of distinct villages in the old style, its effect would be trivial'. On us the effect is baffling—how many villages were there? How related to each other? Did they grow up together or were some later settlements?

Four were enclosed by a wall in Hellenistic times—Pitana, Mesoa, Limnai and Konooura—grouped west, south and east of the low hill which served as an Akropolis, filling the angle between the Eurotas and its tributary, the modern Magoula. It may be that there had never been more. If any had priority it would be Pitana and Mesoa, close to the Akropolis where the earliest pottery has been found. A story of early quarrelling between the pairs over the temple of Artemis Orthia (founded after 900 in Limnai by the Eurotas) would be consistent with the idea that Limnai and Konooura were later foundations; so would the existence of two royal houses in one community.

The story said that these two houses were related. But this cannot be true. Each had a separate burial place, Agiads by the Akropolis, almost certainly in Pitana, Eurypontids to the east in Limnai or Konooura and, besides, the Agiads were known as the senior house. The institution itself (in this form unparalleled in Greece and, as far as I know, elsewhere) and Agiad seniority demand some less fanciful explanation than

the Spartans themselves offered—that the throne was shared by Aristodemos' twins, the elder being determined by a study of the order in
which Aristodemos' queen had bathed her babies. Such an explanation
could be found in the admission of Eurypontids and their followers in
the eastern villages to an already established Spartan state. Indeed two
highly suspicious names appear in the upper reaches of the Eurypontid
genealogy, Prytanis ('President') and Eunomos ('Law-abiding'), easy
inventions to make the two lines match. Delete them and the Eurypontids will begin in the middle of the ninth century, not far from the
date of the earliest pottery from Limnai and the Orthia sanctuary.

There are other questions. What happened to the chiefs of the other
villages? Were there ever four or more kings? Herodotos remarks that
his 'Minyans' demanded at one point to share the kingship so the idea
is not absurd. But all this must be left dark. By 800 B.C. at the latest
there was a united state of at least four villages, ruled by at least two
kings.

Arguments from survivals in later Sparta and by analogy from other
states in Greece, Dorian and non-Dorian, can establish a fairly clear
picture of the society they controlled. Beneath the king was an aristocracy, a handful of men in each of the villages—generals in war,
priests, judges and royal advisers in peacetime—each one of them ruling
his own household and other lesser households, a kind of pyramid
including men from every level of society. Inside each pyramid there
would be clear distinctions of what we should call class; to take the
extremes, between members of the leading family and slaves, but
words we are likely to choose to describe these distinctions, free
farmers, labourers, serfs or the like, have acquired their meanings in a
world in which legal definition is taken for granted and where the
relationship described is usually between a man and his fellows or a
man and society as a whole; in a primitive aristocratic state it is
between a man and those above him, and at the earliest stages it
exists *de facto* rather than *de iure*. Any modern class terms are likely to
be misleading, except perhaps the basic ones, 'free' and 'slave', though
even there it would be hard to say exactly what we mean by 'free'.

This pattern was repeated, with substantial variations of detail,
throughout Greece, and words were coined for the units, the pyramids,
which formed it; the commonest, 'phratry', is used in one late source,
perhaps correctly, of Sparta. There some elements of primitive phratry

life, communal education for the young and the communal life of the adult males, were retained long after they had been lost elsewhere (they also survived in the comparatively isolated Dorian communities of Krete), long enough to have been described, and what we therefore know of them (to be discussed below) gives a valuable, though still only a very partial, glimpse of the complete hold that the early phratry organisation must have had on every department of everyday life.

Inside the phratry the unit was the family; above it stood the tribe, of which in Sparta there were three, the Hylleis, Pamphyloi and Dymanes, and since the same three names are found wherever Dorians appear, the distinction must have grown up in their original common home. From there it may have travelled naturally or it may have been artificially recreated in every new settlement, but in either case, if Sparta's villages were once independent of each other, it seems likely that each would have contained elements, i.e. phratries, of all three tribes, so that any Spartan would be a member of a tribe with fellow-members in the other villages and at the same time a member of a phratry, exclusively rooted in his own village. After the unification he would fight, if he was rich enough to arm and train himself, in his national tribal regiment, but the tribal regiment would be composed of units based on the villages, the phratries. This double criterion is of vital importance in the story of how Spartans slowly came to develop their idea of the 'citizen'.

In Athens and elsewhere the word citizen acquired its content in contrast to the slave (and of course the foreigner). In Sparta slaves played no part but there were other politically depressed classes who offered no less of a contrast—roughly the whole population of Laconia and Messenia outside Sparta itself and its immediate environs, a population divided in later centuries into two very different groups, *perioikoi* and helots. The *perioikos* was a citizen of the internally largely autonomous communities of which there was a fair number in the more distant parts of Laconia and Messenia, most of them on the coast, a few inland nearer Sparta. As such he had whatever rights his city might accord him and, as an individual, theoretically no obligations to Sparta; as such he could be rich or poor, aristocrat, farmer, artisan or merchant. But his city did have obligations, to provide troops for Sparta's wars, to accept any decisions that Sparta might take for them; its authority was entirely restricted to matters of local administration and even there some Spartan interference is attested (there was a Spartan magistrate in perioikic Kythera during the fifth century and under certain circumstances Spartan officials could put *perioikoi* to death without a trial). Still, the politically unambitious *perioikos* could be a happy man.

It is less easy to picture a happy helot. The word itself is probably derived from the root *Hel-* implying seizure or capture and the vast majority of first generation helots must have owed their position to the common Greek practice of enslaving a defeated enemy. But there the similarity ends. Elsewhere, in general, a slave was the property of his master; the helot belonged to the Spartan state, assigned by the state to an individual master but not disposable by him. Again elsewhere the slave could frequently acquire his freedom; except in extraordinary circumstances the helot could not. Thus he was at once freer and more constrained than his fellows in the rest of Greece. Indeed with an absentee landlord, as all Spartans were, the life of many may not in practice have been much different from that of poorer peasants elsewhere. But although this freedom and comparative prosperity might lessen the urge to revolt, their numbers, the permanence of the breed, and their national identity (most were of Messenian origin) made them an ever present menace to Sparta's security.

But these are descriptions of the *perioikos* and helot of classical Sparta; for the creation of the classes we must look back to the years of Sparta's first expansion in Laconia. Here there were fewer urban centres down to about 750 than there had been in the thirteenth century. But the population had grown since 1200 and some villages, even towns, must have appeared to house it. It would be no surprise if Sparta, in the richest part of the plain, developed faster than the rest, nor, since it shared that plain with well-established Amyklai, five miles to the south, if its first attempts at expansion were to the north. To ninth-century kings Pausanias ascribes campaigns in Kynouria, over the north end of Parnon; more plausibly to Archelaos and Charillos (together in the second quarter of the eighth) the annexation of the area towards the headwaters of the Eurotas. But much more important is the first move southwards 'in the reign of Teleklos . . . not long before the Messenian War', i.e. between about 750 and 740. Then Pharis, Geronthrai and Amyklai were seized—the first two without a struggle, Amyklai after a desperate siege—probably the only three centres of any importance north of the ridge which divides Sparta from the sea.

For Pharis and Geronthrai we have only Pausanias' story: the towns were taken, their people fled, we are not told where, and Spartans occupied Geronthrai as colonists. But Sparta and Amyklai had long been neighbours; their relations were no doubt complicated in fact— from the tangled tradition they are unrecoverable. Pausanias again is straightforward; siege, capture, expulsion, once for all in Teleklos' reign. But other sources tell other stories, of Amyklaian collaboration with the first Dorian invaders, of subjection by these invaders, of subjection followed by later revolt, of Amyklaians in flight to Krete, Kypros and elsewhere. It can only be said that stories of early conflict or contact could have been invented to fit the general belief in an instantaneous Dorian subjugation of Laconia, whereas no comparable doubt attaches to the tale of an eighth-century war. Since others besides Pausanias admit a longish period of Amyklaian co-existence with Sparta, that much may be taken as firm; to trust his precise date for the final showdown is more venturesome but it makes a reasonable story. Amyklai, then, would have been captured around 750 and, once captured, was not treated like the more distant Pharis or Geronthrai; together with any inhabitants who remained it was incorporated into the Spartan state.

As mistress of the upper Eurotas valley Sparta could expand in any of four directions; northwards into the Arkadian hills; across Parnon into Kynouria where she would have to face a tough Dorian rival in Argos whose influence already extended southwards along the coast as far as Malea and the island of Kythera; southwards to the sea where again she might meet Argos; or into Messenia, the richest prize of all. She chose Messenia and, still in Teleklos' reign, colonists were sent across Taygetos to three sites in the Nedon valley; a little later, about 740, Teleklos was murdered, by Messenians the Spartans said, and this became one excuse for a full-scale war of annexation which introduced Sparta for the first time to the wider Greek world and, more significantly, to the problems which were to govern her history for centuries to come.

But first to end the story of Laconia. With the capture of Amyklai Spartan influence must have spread quickly southwards, peacefully perhaps, for there is no record of a campaign against any of the coastal cities except Helos at the north-east corner of the Gulf which had Argive backing. This was reduced by force in (Pausanias again) the reign of King Alkamenes, c. 740 to c. 700, and here a new feature appears—the people of Helos suffered the same fate as the Messenians suffered (c. 715), they were enslaved as Helots (some Greek scholars saw here the origin of the name).

It may only be coincidence that stories of colonisation, to Geronthrai and the Nedon valley, or of incorporation (Amyklai) should be followed after 740 by these two cases of enslavement, but it could mark a readily intelligible change of policy. The Eurotas valley north of Amyklai contained under fifty square miles of cultivable ground, enough for two thousand families or so with their dependents, but hardly enough to meet the needs of that expansion of population which more settled conditions were bringing to the whole of Greece; small wonder if Spartans were ready to abandon Sparta for new fields in conquered territory even if it meant becoming a Geronthriate or a Nedonian. So Romans in the early second century were ready to lose their citizenship in exchange for membership of a Latin colony. But just as Roman citizenship gradually came to mean more than a few acres in the Po valley (no Latin colonies were sent out after 183), so when Sparta's first desperate need for land was satisfied (Teleklos' activity must have nearly doubled her territory) the motive for further expansion became greed, not hunger, and the greed could only be satisfied by remaining a Spartan—Geronthriates would not be given land in Messenia. Moreover there is a limit to the amount of land one man can work; for her new acres Sparta needed not only Spartan owners but a non-Spartan labour force. Hence, I would guess, the treatment meted out to the men of Helos and Messenia, not necessarily new treatment—there may well have been men in Laconia before 715 who found themselves bound to Sparta in a helot-like relationship—but newly applied on a wide scale to solve a new economic problem.

Meanwhile colonisation had set the pattern for the development of the perioikic cities. Had Geronthrai prospered famously we might one day have seen a perioikic Sparta, but it was Sparta which prospered and this superiority, coupled with the natural authority of a mother-city, would soon reduce the colonies to complete obedience. And so, as the Spartan gradually won greater influence in the government of his own city, he also won an indirect voice in the control of *perioikoi*; whatever domestic political power the Geronthriate might win, he would still have no say in the government of Sparta.

It must be added, however, that many perioikic cities were not in origin colonies. In the course of her expansion Sparta must often have found it to her advantage to come to terms with, rather than destroy other Dorian or non-Dorian communities; in some cases the agreement may have been as between equals, in others Spartan superiority may have been recognised from the start; either way these 'allies' will soon have found themselves on the same path as the colonists to complete subjection. Then again, once the relationship had developed naturally for colonist or ally it soon became, like *Latinitas* in Italy, a status that could be artificially formalised and deliberately bestowed. In later times Sparta could create a perioikic city by decree as and when it suited her.

BIBLIOGRAPHY

Early Greek aristocratic society: M. I. Finley, *The World of Odysseus* (1954); more briefly my *Emergence of Greek Democracy* (1966) ch. II; A. Andrewes, *Hermes 89* (1961) 129 ff.

Amyklai: F. Kiechle, *Lakonien und Sparta* (1963) chs. I.4 and II.1.

Perioikoi: J. A. O. Larsen, Pauly-Wissowa *Real-Enzyklopaedie* s.v.; F. Gschitzner, *Abhängige Orte* (1958) 61 ff.

Helots: D. Lotze, Μεταξὺ ἐλευθέρων καὶ δούλων (1959).

4

SPARTA AND THE OUTSIDE WORLD

Sparta's chief Dorian rival, Argos, had done rather more than Sparta before 750 to achieve in fact the position which tradition gave to the brother Temenos in the first partition of the Peloponnese. The greater part of the north-east Peloponnese was 'dorianised' from Argos and she had won some kind of control over the whole eastern coastal strip. At the same time she was far more absorbed in the world at large than was isolated Laconia—when her neighbours, Korinth and Aigina, the latter probably still an Argive dependency, turned their attention to the sea during the eighth century Argos herself cannot have stayed wholly aloof.

Tensions produced elsewhere by Greek expansion led, in the second half of the eighth century, to a major war, the so-called Lelantine War, between the Euboian cities of Chalkis and Eretria, a war in which, Thucydides says, the greater part of the Greek world became involved. Our evidence limits the known contestants to Korinth and Samos on the side of Chalkis; Megara, Miletos and Chios on the side of Eretria, but this is not the 'greater part of the Greek world' and it would be strange if Aigina and consequently Argos were not drawn in. If so it would be as allies of Eretria and there is one story of an early, but undatable, attack by Eretria's enemy, Samos, on Aigina.

On the face of it Sparta's invasion of Messenia, c. 735–715, need have no connection with this other war, for Messenia was just as remote as Sparta itself from the mainstream of Greek affairs. But there are clear signs that it was part of the wider pattern. Messenian friends of Sparta

were given a home in Chalkis' colony at Rhegion in South Italy and
perhaps some indirect help by Korinth; even distant Samos, Herodotos
says, once sent support to Sparta against the Messenians, probably in
this war, and another undated but early campaign is recorded, by
Eretria's ally Miletos against Sparta's colony Melos (below p. 38).

Argos, of course, provides the link between Sparta's local struggle
and the Aegean world: Argos as an ally of Eretria against Sparta, friend
of Chalkis. Hence the otherwise surprising fact that on one, perhaps
two, occasions during the Messenian War we find Sparta's attention
diverted to her eastern frontier. The attack on Argive-supported Helos
in Alkamenes' reign (*c.* 740–*c.* 700) may have come after the war, but
in the middle of it, towards 720, a Spartan army under King Nikander
(*c.* 750–*c.* 720), with help from Argos' neighbour Asine, ravaged the
Argolid. Shortly afterwards the Argives took their revenge by destroying Asine, and at this point our source, Pausanias, has the support of
archaeology—Asine was destroyed around 700 B.C.

It is impossible to know what kind of coherence we should try to
impose on the war as a whole—was Nikander's invasion part of a
'Chalkidian' plan or a random sortie, was the Samian help against
Messenia an expeditionary force or a passing Samian ship? Or on its
outcome—Chalkis seems to have won in Euboia but across the Aegean
Miletos seems to have got the better of Samos. For Sparta, however, the
result was triumph. Helos was captured and, much more important,
Messenia was crushed.

The archaeological history of Messenia is not unlike that of Laconia;
destruction around 1200, scattered survivors thereafter, a few new
settlements with the beginning of proto-geometric chiefly around the
Messenian Gulf in the plain of modern Kalamata. Again we assume
Dorian newcomers but no once-for-all Dorian kingdom (even the
tradition allows an admixture of Arkadian blood in the Messenian
royal house). Rather a number of more or less separate, more or less
Dorian, more or less weak or powerful units. Geographically there are
five natural divisions, Pylos, modern Kyparissia, the middle and upper
Pamisos valley (the plain of Stenyklaros), the west coast of the gulf
where one major proto-geometric site has been found at Nichoria, and
finally in the plain between the Pamisos and the Nedon. But there is
no knowing how far geography was reflected in the political organisation.

Of these areas Stenyklaros was Sparta's immediate prize. She approached it probably from the north-east, around Taygetos, rather than from her existing possessions on the Nedon, and it was won twenty years later, says Tyrtaios, when the Messenians 'abandoned their rich fields and took to flight from the great mountains of Ithome', the range which flanked the valley on the west. For the moment Spartan arms may not have been carried further west, to Pylos or Kyparissia, even the settlements around the lower Pamisos and down the coast of the gulf kept a nominal independence.

But it was only nominal. Some communities may already have come to terms, others followed and the whole area became largely, if not entirely, perioikic. By about 700 Sparta's control was firm enough to let her settle her old allies of Asine in a new town near Cape Akritas and perhaps others of her friends elsewhere. The reasons for this difference of approach (in itself one of the strongest arguments for believing the tradition that Stenyklaros was the objective) are obscure. Perhaps some of these southern communities were already strong enough to make alliance seem more politic than straight aggression; conceivably they contained a more substantial Dorian element for whom common blood might earn easier treatment; maybe there was already more widespread Spartan infiltration in the area than we have supposed (Pherai, modern Kalamata, is said to have been a Spartan colony). But whatever the reason the fact is clear; collaboration of a sort in the south, conquest in the north, followed by the annexation of Messenia's land and the enslavement of her people.

Some Messenians, says Tyrtaios, left their lands and fled; to friendly Arkadia and elsewhere, adds Pausanias, an obvious enough guess. But the bulk of the population remained behind, the raw material from which was fashioned, by natural development or later deliberate modification, the classical helot. Tyrtaios sketches their position: 'like asses under a heavy burden they were constrained to carry to their masters a half of all the harvest that the fields might bear', and 'they and their wives as well must put on mourning and bewail their lords whenever death should carry one away' (I adopt here an interpretation of Tyrtaios fragments 4 and 5 which makes them contrast the fate of those Messenians who fled and those who stayed. This is justified, I think, by the setting in which Pausanias quotes them).

The rules which Tyrtaios states are precise enough but hardly complete, and only guesswork can provide the rest. In guessing we must guard against two anachronistic ideas. First that there could be anything like an army of occupation for the new territory or even any very full Spartan system of administration—to some extent Messenians must have tended to their own affairs. Second that the land could at this date have been parcelled out in small lots among a host of individual Spartans—the 9,000 or so 'Equals' who made up later Sparta did not yet exist. If there was direct allotment it will have been to a comparatively small number of the already privileged; one thinks rather of a disorganised scramble.

On the other hand Tyrtaios makes it sound as if Sparta's relations were with individual Messenians, not with anything we could call a Messenian state, while in another fragment he encourages Spartans to fight at the time of Messenia's seventh-century revolt by reminding them that it is 'good to plant and good to plough Messenia'—surely a suggestion that many of them already had a direct interest in Messenian soil, consequently a hint that direct exploitation had been the method from the start. In short, I am inclined to think that it is right to talk of annexation and enslavement, but in doing so we must remember that both words may be misleading.

However that may be, the consequences of Sparta's victory determined her history for three centuries and more. The rest of Greece had felt the same need for land, but most major cities had looked for it in colonies overseas. At the same time some of those left at home had turned from farming to trade or manufacture, more and more as exchange developed between colony and colony, or colony and homeland. The resultant economic revolution was twofold: the community grew richer, the wealth was no longer exclusively agricultural. Sparta too became richer, vastly richer, and did so even more suddenly than the others, but her new wealth was in land alone and in land on her own frontiers. At one stroke she had committed herself to an almost purely agricultural future and robbed herself of the common incentive to look outside her own borders. One colony she did send out in 708 to Tarentum, but this was a special case; earlier she had taken a hand in settling Thera, Melos and perhaps some cities in Krete, but all of these were before 750 and may have been early enough to belong to the time of post-migration disturbance rather than that of settled expansion. In any case none drew her attention abroad.

Then, to exploit the new wealth, Sparta had equipped herself with a large non-Spartan labour force, inferior enough to breed resentment which, sharpened by nationalist and racial hatred, Messenian against Spartan, non-Dorian against Dorian, and fostered by generation after generation of common experience, diverted more and more of Sparta's energy to the ugly and difficult task of holding her place as mistress of the South Peloponnese. Sparta could be adventurous, but even at her most adventurous she could never act without a backward glance for trouble at home and at any setback there were voices raised to argue that security in the Peloponnese was more vital to her interests than any prize she might acquire abroad.

Until the battle of Leuktra in 371 her policy was largely controlled by thoughts of the profits and the dangers she had incurred by the conquest of Messenia. And even then, like the shadow of Taygetos which falls on the Eurotas early in a summer evening while the eastern hills are still hot in the sunshine, the loss of Messenia brought a chill despondency to the rest of Sparta's history. She should have felt relief at the end of her responsibility but by then she was too set in her ways to look for another road to prosperity.

BIBLIOGRAPHY

The Lelantine War: W. G. Forrest, *Historia 6* (1957) 160 ff.; cf. and contrast J. Boardman, *BSA 52* (1957) 27 ff.
Messenian archaeology and the Messenian myth: see bibliography to ch. I.
Greek expansion: T. J. Dunbabin, *Greeks and their Eastern Neighbours* (1957); J. Boardman, *The Greeks Overseas* (1964).

EXCURSUS I

THE LYKOURGAN REFORMS

Classical Sparta was renowned for the skill and courage of her army and for the stability and excellence of her constitution. Both, it was thought, she owed to the genius of one man, Lykourgos, who, far back in her history, had created all those institutions which made Sparta and the Spartans what they were. There was a large element of myth in this simple picture: Lykourgos adapted as much as he created and much of what he produced had been altered or even superseded long before fifth- or fourth-century scholars began to study their contemporary 'Lykourgan' Sparta; Lykourgos himself is a shadowy, possibly even a mythical figure—those same scholars found less evidence for his life than for his works; and the antiquity of his system has been grossly exaggerated. And yet the picture has substantial elements of truth in it: at some stage the Spartan state was drastically overhauled; this overhaul did come as early as if not earlier than similar changes elsewhere and Sparta for the most part did avoid those upheavals which later destroyed the work of other early constitution-mongers; and in a world where individual law-givers abounded but revolution by committee is unknown the chances are that Sparta too owed her new look to a single hand.

But the attempt to separate truth from myth leaves such a wide area of doubt and the dating of the changes is so uncertain that it would be misleading to discuss them in the course of a narrative history. This excursus is therefore designed to set out the problems as fairly as I can, to show where the narrative of the following chapters can be justified and to indicate how it would have to be altered if we gave different answers.

(A) THE NATURE OF THE REFORMS

In a chapter of his *Life of Lykourgos* which probably derives from Aristotle, Plutarch quotes 'an oracle which the Spartans call a *rhetra* (an enactment)'. The language of the text which follows has poetic, even oracular, touches; on the other hand its provisions were undoubtedly observed in the later Spartan constitution. So, we suppose, a law based on an oracle or, as I should prefer, an oracle which was acted on; either way, a vital part of the Lykourgan legislation and by far the most authoritative evidence for it.

Its text, translated with, I hope, a minimum of prejudice and dogma, is as follows:

> I (a) When a sanctuary of Zeus Sullanios and Athena Sullania has been established,
> (b) the people divided into tribes and *obai*
> (c) and thirty men, including the kings, appointed as a *Gerousia* [Senate].
> II The Apellai [a feast of Apollo] shall be celebrated from time to time between Babyka and Knakion.
> III Thus questions shall be introduced and withdrawals made.
> IV To the assembly of the citizens shall also be given the final authority.
> V [according to Plutarch a later amendment] If the people speaks crookedly, the elders [*sc.* the *Gerousia*] and the kings shall be setters-aside.

In the Greek the verbs (participles in Clause I, infinitives elsewhere) are active in form but no subject is stated—a feature of early Greek documentary style best rendered in English by using passives so that each verb can be left to take its own perhaps quite separate subject from the context, readily obvious to Spartans if not to us.

I (a) Although the epithets of Zeus and Athena, if properly transmitted, are not otherwise known, the attempt to guarantee the

approval of heaven for the new order is common Greek practice and
need not delay us.

I (b) Here there are two problems, what were the tribes and *obai*
and how were they related? The tribes were almost certainly the original
Dorian three, the Hylleis, Pamphyloi and Dymanes; the word *oba*,
whatever its origin, meant in practice those 'villages' which, as
Thucydides said, made up the Spartan state. Four of these, Limnai,
Konooura, Pitana and Mesoa, were enclosed by the Hellenistic city-
wall, and with a fifth whose members were called *Neopolitai* ('new-
citizens'—no doubt a later creation) these were probably all that were
left to the truncated Sparta of the Roman occupation, all therefore
that were likely to earn a mention in what is the main body of our
evidence for Sparta's internal structure, inscriptions of the Roman
period. But one random stone from Amyklai shows that it too had
once had obal status, and the garbled text of another (the stone itself
is lost) seems to name one more, the Arkaloi or Argaloi. Other names
could be guessed from chance references to mythical figures who
might have been eponymous obal heroes or to places around Sparta
which might have been *obai* and there are traces on the ground of three
or four substantial villages within a mile or two of the city, villages too
close to have had the independent life of a perioikic community, which
might therefore have been obal centres. But all these are guesses. The
original number of the *obai* cannot be recovered. It was not less than
five (the central four with Amyklai), probably not less than six (adding
the Arkaloi), and may well have been more.

The figure five did figure in some areas of Spartan organisation—
most strikingly the chief magistrates, the ephors, were five in number
and a fragment of Aristotle's *Constitution* may have asserted that the
Spartan army at some stage fought in five *lochoi* (companies)—and this
has led many scholars to accept the smallest figure.

But although the Spartan army was indeed based on the *obai* after
the reforms and the word *lochos* is once used of an obal contingent
(Herodotos mentions a *lochos* of Pitana at Pilataia in 479), there were
drastic changes before Aristotle's day and from one brief sentence out
of context there is no way of telling either to what period Aristotle
referred his *lochoi* or whether he was writing of an army made up of five
units or of five particular units in a larger force. Moreover he names his

lochoi and only one of them bears any resemblance to those of the five certain *obai*. As for the ephors, in Sparta's colony, Thera, and Thera's colony, Kyrene, their number for long was three, matching the three Dorian tribes, but this might indicate either a correlation with the main social unit at any time, i.e. that in Sparta five ephors implied five units, five *obai*, or a correlation with the three Dorian tribes, i.e. that in origin there were three ephors in Sparta whose number was raised at some later date for some special reason, for example at the unknown moment when it was ruled that two ephors should always accompany the king on campaign.

There is besides one positive argument against the theory of five *obai*. The Spartan citizen body numbered some 9,000 men, nearly 2,000 for each of five *obai*, with a minimum of slaves and family, a population of not less than 10,000 per *oba*. But the total area inside the city wall was roughly half a mile square and if we allow for the Akropolis and the Agora, for public buildings and for the open space needed to give each of the four urban units its 'village' look, 100,000 square yards would seem to be a fair figure for each, for its own temples, public places and its population. Ten square yards per soul is not a very generous allowance. Greeks did not live in tenements.

The next question is the relationship of tribe and *oba*. The latter had existed before the reform; for all we know it may even have had some formal recognition as part of the state organisation. But whereas the primitive Spartan army had fought in three tribal units (this is asserted by Tyrtaios) her later army was drawn up by *obai*. Lykourgos then must either have recognised the *obai* for the first time or have given them a far greater prominence than they had before. To do so he must either have accepted two independent classifications of the citizen body, one by birth, the other by residence, or he must somehow have integrated the two.

Pointing to an apparent parallel in Attika where the old Ionian tribes were left intact when new local tribes were created in 508, many have opted for two registers. But this is unlikely. In Attika the old tribes survived as religious associations, they played no part in public life; here, mentioned in an organisational document alongside the all-important *obai*, they must mean something more than a sentimental reverence for a tribal past. But, if so, the double classification is quite unparalleled elsewhere in Greece and the 'something more' which they represented defies speculation.

Integration then. But how? An *oba* could not be a subdivision of a tribe unless the whole population of, say, Pitana was prepared to be rechristened, say, Dymanes overnight, a drastic and one would think unwelcome move (sentiment does count for something). Nor with three tribes and at least five *obai* could a tribe be a subdivision of an *oba*. Somehow the classifications must cut across each other and when we remember the physical pattern of early Dorian settlement and the peculiarities of Dorian society the method that must have been used is easily seen.

Even after the conquest of Messenia the Spartan lived in his village, his *oba*, not on his estates; the early family or 'phratry' in Pitana would tend to remain a family or 'phratry' in Pitana, its stability further reinforced by those communal institutions of primitive Dorians for which the phratry acted as a focus (below p. 51 ff). But each phratry in turn belonged as a unit to one of the three tribes, and, given a mixed bag of settlers for each village at the start, chances are that one or more 'phratries' of Hylleis, Pamphyloi and Dymanes would be found in every village. To ignore these existing units in a reorganisation of the army would be pointless; simply to reallocate them to new local regiments would make excellent sense. Why should a phratry of Dymanes in Amyklai march several miles to train with other Dymanes in Pitana when it could so easily cross the road and train with Hylleis and Pamphyloi in its own Amyklai? A Spartan already belonged to a group which had both tribal and local affiliations. Why waste the material that lay to hand when shifting the emphasis from one to the other?

Some readjustment would no doubt be necessary but in principle there could have been three tribal units inside each *oba*. There is some slender evidence that there were. In a very fragmentary commentary on the poet Alkman, who, I shall argue, wrote after the reform, the words Pitana and Dymainai (feminine of Dymanes) occur in the same context, as if, for example, a chorus of the Dymainai of Pitana had been mentioned by the poet, and elsewhere the commentator seems to assert that there existed something called a *patra* of Dymanes—and *patra* is a word closely akin to phratry (though usually applied to a smaller unit). More explicitly, a Hellenistic scholar, Demetrios of

Skepsis, described the organisation of the Karneian games at Sparta as 'a reflection of the military training system', a system which we should expect after the reforms as it was still in Roman times to be based on the *oba*. In this 'reflection', Demetrios says, each major unit (each *oba*?) was made up of three 'phratries' (one for each of the Dorian tribes?) and there were nine major units in all (nine *obai*?—a plausible number).

My hypothesis then is this—nine local *obai* so constructed from twenty-seven tribal phratries that the Spartan in his assembly could stand, as the *rhetra* seems to imply he stood, both with his fellow tribesmen and with his fellow obesman, to his left and his right the other Hylleis, in front and behind the other Amyklaians. According to later tradition Lykourgos created a citizen body of 9,000 men (an active army, therefore, of something over 6,000) and since Herodotos gives 8,000 for the citizen population in 480 the tradition may well be correct—1,000 men per *oba* (about 700 for its regiment), 330 men per phratry (230 for its company).

But other elements too, social and military, would have to be fitted into any final picture, the *lochos*, the *mora* and three military institutions ascribed by Herodotos to Lykourgos—the *enomotia*, the *triakas* and the *sussition*. The *mora*, the *lochos* and the *enomotia* all existed in the reorganised army of the late fifth century (below p. 132 ff.), with paper strengths of 640, of 320 and of forty respectively, the *enomotia* being made up of one member from each of the forty year-classes eligible for military service. For the earlier army the *mora* is not attested at all but may none the less have existed, the *enomotia* is mentioned only by Herodotos and the same author writes of a *lochos* based on the *oba* of Pitana at Plataia in 479. Thucydides on the other hand denies the existence of such a unit. The Herodotean *Ttriakas*, a word which could mean thirty men, thirty families, or a thirtieth of something, is not otherwise attested for Sparta, but as a social unit it occurs in Kos where it numbered something between 100 and 500 men.

Finally the *sussitia*, the famous common-messes at which all Spartans had to eat. A social institution of course, but also, as Herodotos says, a part of the military system and as such surely each *sussition* must have been the basis of one military unit. But although the habits of a *sussition* are well enough attested (below p. 52 ff.) its size is not. According to Plutarch it had a mere fifteen members but when Agis IV set out to recreate the 'Lykourgan' system in the third century B.C. he proposed *sussitia* of an average of 300. The former figure is impossibly small, the latter surprisingly but not outrageously large and, since the similar messes of Dorian Krete were common to a whole phratry, I am inclined to think that the same may have been true of Sparta; on my hypothesis of a phratry's size, it seems that on this point Agis had not lost touch with the past.

If we can accept that a *sussition* was the mess of such a phratry; if further we can explain the quarrel between Herodotos and Thucydides about the *lochos* of Pitana as a misunderstanding by supposing that Herodotos meant not the one and only *lochos* but 'the lochos of which I am speaking, in fact one of three *lochoi* of Pitana', we get the equation: phratry=*sussition* (when eating)=*lochos* (when fighting), and, without violating any of the evidence, could offer the following table:

SOCIAL UNIT	STRENGTH	MILITARY UNIT	STRENGTH
The *damos* (the people)	9,000	the *stratos* (the army)	6,500
Oba	1,000	? *mora*	720
Phratry (? *patra*)			
=*sussition*	330	*lochos*	240
? *triakas* (one thirtieth of a tribe of 3,000)	110	? *triakas*	80
?	55	*enomotia*	40

But this is intended only to illustrate the sort of structure we may imagine; it must not be taken as any more than the guess that it is.

I (c) No foundation of the *Gerousia* is in question. There must always have been a Royal Council of a sort in Sparta; at most it is to be reorganised, at least it is to have its number fixed by rule—thirty including the two kings. There was a tradition that Lykourgos chose the first members himself but later, if not in fact from the start, there was election, limited to candidates over sixty years of age from a prescribed group of aristocratic families, election by a method which seemed to Aristotle childish and to us either ludicrous or crooked (a hidden panel of judges tried to estimate the volume of applause given to each contestant by the assembly). The senator, once chosen, served for life and was not responsible for his acts to any outside authority. Given this irresponsibility, the prestige of the individual members and the accumulated prestige of the institution, the authority of this body—like that of any similar aristocratic council elsewhere, the Roman Senate, for example—was enormous, quite apart from any specific powers it may have had. But even its specific powers were wide enough. Judicially it seems to have controlled all the more important of what we should call criminal cases; politically, as the rest of the *rhetra* will show, it controlled virtually everything.

II Thus a regular popular assembly is guaranteed, the most striking provision of the whole document. The frequency of its meetings will depend on the frequency of the Apellai which is unknown, perhaps once a month with one more important celebration annually in the month which carried Apollo's name, Apellaios, the occasion for elections and the like. Similarly the place of assembly escapes us but Spartans would not have needed Aristotle's unhelpful comment that Babyka was a bridge and Knakion a river.

III In the standard constitution of the developed Greek state there was a sovereign assembly, whether oligarchically or democratically constituted; there was also, invariably, a smaller body, again chosen in a variety of ways, which acted partly as an executive, partly as an independent administrator in matters too small for the assembly's attention, and partly as what the Greeks called a 'probouleutic' body for the assembly, i.e. as a forum for the preparation of an agenda, for preliminary discussion of the issues, often for the formulation of positive proposals to be put to the larger body. In Sparta these functions belonged to the *Gerousia* which must therefore be understood as the agent in the first part of this clause. 'Subjects shall be introduced to the assembly by the *Gerousia*.' But what can be meant by 'withdrawals shall be made'?

The verb used can mean either 'stand aside' or 'set aside' and from the same root comes the noun 'setters-aside' in the amendment (clause V). The two processes must then be closely related if not identical, but if identical the *Gerousia* cannot be the understood subject in clause III since it is the stated subject in clause V and in that case the amendment would not amend. Either the subject or the process implied must change.

This rules out several popular translations, for example, 'The *Gerousia* shall introduce proposals and *adjourn proceedings* [i.e. set the assembly aside] . . . the *Gerousia* shall *adjourn proceedings.*' For if what looks like an identical right of adjournment was in fact different the difference should be made clear in the Greek. Other translations avoid this objection; for example, 'Proposals shall be introduced (by the *Gerousia*) and decisions reached (by the people who *stand aside* from a question because they have settled it) . . . the *Gerousia* shall reach a decision (without the people)'. But none of these is entirely satisfactory. In the example quoted the sense is admirable but it gives a meaning to the verb ('reach a decision') which is unparalleled and a long way from the basic 'stand (or set) aside'.

Recorded procedure at two later meetings of the Spartan assembly, however, point the way to a different interpretation. In these, one just after the Persian Wars, the other in the third century, the *Gerousia* seems to meet twice, once before, once after the assembly, and to formulate its decision in the light of (in neither case in accordance with) the assembly's wishes. Its decision reached, in one case the assembly meets again to ratify it, in the other it is not consulted. Could these second meetings of the *Gerousia* be the 'withdrawals' of the *rhetra*? 'Questions [rather than proposals] shall be introduced by the *Gerousia* and after discussion the *Gerousia* shall *stand aside* to reconsider the question in the light of the discussion and subsequently, if it sees fit, submit a proposal to a reconvened assembly for ratification . . . but if the assembly speaks crookedly the *Gerousia* shall *set* it *aside* and reach a decision on its own.' The four stages here posited, introduction of an issue, discussion, formulation, decision, are of course implicit in any legislative process, even if in practice the first and third are often combined and, when they are not, the formulation is usually left to emerge in the course of the discussion. The assumption that they were originally distinct at Sparta is not a difficult one.

IV This clause might well have settled the problem, had its text been sound. As it is, the first few words are garbled nonsense and some surgery is needed. Most modern scholars have agreed that two rights are being given to the citizen body, the right of meeting (and/or of speaking) and of decision. But there are difficulties. The right to meet is already explicit in clauses II and III, perhaps the right of discussion as well, and the document is not on the whole repetitious. Besides Aristotle in the *Politics* denies that the Spartan assembly could discuss a proposal (N.B. a proposal) put to it by the *Gerousia*, they could but listen and vote. Both difficulties can be avoided by following up my suggestion for clause III with a slightly different cure to the corruption of clause IV. 'To the assembly of the citizen-body shall also be given the final decision' i.e. after the withdrawal the *Gerousia* shall announce a proposal to the assembly and take a vote. At this second meeting there is to be no discussion.

V The ban on discussion, to be more precise the ban on discussion which might lead to an alteration of the proposal rather than simple rejection, could be the result of this clause. 'If the people speaks crookedly . . .', literally 'if it utters a crooked *rhetra* . . .'. 'Crooked' is often understood to mean simply 'wrong in the eyes of the *Gerousia*'. In other words if the *Gerousia* does not like the popular decision it ignores it. But politically meek though the Spartans were, they cannot have been as meek as this, and 'crooked' is much better taken as 'distorted', by amendment or counter-proposal from the floor—I should like to add, after the *Gerousia* has presented a formal motion.

The legislative process which clause V completes may well have been modified in later practice but no further legislation is recorded. The behaviour of any later assembly, and any other evidence there may be, should be explicable in terms of the *rhetra*'s rules. As we have seen two such assemblies are, others do not conflict; other evidence is limited to Plutarch's brief and incomplete commentary on the text which the above interpretation follows closely, and to the passage of Aristotle's *Politics* already cited.

There, as well as denying the assembly any right of counter-proposal, Aristotle implies that it could not even challenge the agenda initially prepared by the *Gerousia* if the *Gerousia* itself was unanimous, and altogether paints a much more docile gathering than the assembly of the *rhetra* or of later fact would seem to be. But with both of these bars to popular freedom everything would depend on the spirit in which they were interpreted—armed with them, unscrupulous chairmanship could easily turn the assembly into a farcical nonentity; but how unscrupulous was the *Gerousia*? On the other hand, while it retained the right of discussion at the earlier stage (which Aristotle omits but certainly existed), an excited and determined assembly could just as easily make its opinion felt; but how often was the assembly excited? The surviving evidence is for moments of crisis, of excitement; Aristotle's evidence, presumably, included much of the day-to-day routine where even discussion may have been scarcely noticeable. We simply cannot grasp the real atmosphere of later political life under the *rhetra*'s rules.

For the time of its formulation things are clearer. There would always have been an assembly at Sparta, an assembly not unlike the gathering of the Greek army before Troy as Homer describes it in the *Iliad*, summoned to hear the sometimes far from united views of its princes, able perhaps to influence those princes by its reactions. The assembly envisaged by the men who framed the *rhetra* will have been of much the same type with two vital differences. Its meetings were to be regular and, after the *Gerousia* had reached a decision in the light of the 'debate', this decision had to be announced to and approved by the same assembly. But we may suppose, as Plutarch following Aristotle does, that the assembly proved more enterprising than had been expected, that either in the preliminary discussion or in the final vote it managed on occasions to thwart its princes' views, to make the enactments 'crooked'. And so a right, the right of counter-proposal, which had not been explicitly denied in the terms of the *rhetra* (because it had not been imagined) was formally withdrawn.

The *rhetra* is a constitutional document, incidentally relevant to the military organisation. For the rest of Lykourgos' work we have to turn to more detailed but less reliable evidence, the mass of tradition which hung around the reformer's name and of which Plutarch's *Life* probably gives a fair sample. It was claimed, for example, that Lykourgos banned the use of coined money, remarkable prescience in a statesman who at the latest of the many dates proposed for him lived half a century before any Spartan would have dreamed of coinage. Other 'Lykourgan' prescriptions are no less suspicious but less easy to check—did he forbid the use of any tools but an axe and a saw in the building of a house?—and common sense is usually the only guide to what Lykourgos himself is likely to have done in creating the three great Spartan characteristics of which tradition saw him as the deliberate author— equality among Spartans, military fitness and efficiency, and austerity.

The citizens of Sparta were known as *Homoioi*—'Equals', a word which clearly implies an earlier state of inequality and a deliberate act of creation. Two possible areas of inequality suggest themselves and two appropriate acts are recorded; the *rhetra* by implication guarantees equal political rights as members of the assembly; and secondly the tradition unanimously ascribed to Lykourgos the introduction of equal allotments of land (*kleroi*) to all citizens. Much about this land allotment is obscure but the principal feature of later practice, the official grant of a *kleros*, Plutarch says by the elders of the phratry to a child at birth, to be held inalienably for life, is not likely to be the result of random development—for one thing it would require the setting aside of something like a quarter of a million acres of public land. Such things smack of revolution and Lykourgos is by far the most likely revolutionary.

But in both these respects the equality was unreal. Only a few were even eligible for the *Gerousia*; everyone had his public *kleros* but there was also private land in Sparta where private enterprise produced its usual consequences—there may have been no paupers among the *Homoioi* but there were some wealthy men, some very wealthy. 'Equality' therefore is an odd word to use when in fact it means no more than 'not falling below a certain minimum in two respects' and we must look for a wider area and a more genuine content. There is no need to look far. Lykourgos vastly enlarged, if he did not create, for Spartans the idea of being a citizen and an essential element in this idea was the equality of all citizens, not as human beings but as citizens. As a citizen the Spartan had an equal *kleros* from which he supported what was in many respects a standard way of life, he had an equal standing in the eyes of the law, an equal claim to any right the state might choose to give; in return an equal duty to submit to the laws and to serve the state as it might require. In this context the private fortune of a few is irrelevant and against this wider background of political equality even the public political privilege of a few aristocrats would seem unimportant.

By far the most important duty imposed by the state was submission to Lykourgos' second great invention, the *agoge* or system of military training. The baby whom the elders of the phratry rejected at birth was abandoned to die; some might think him lucky, for after six years with his mother, the child who had been accepted was taken from home and enrolled in a group of his contemporaries under the leadership of an older boy. Details of the organisation are even harder to unravel than those of the army but are not very important. What we know for sure is that with his group the boy lived for the next fourteen years as he worked his way up through the increasingly brutal and brutalising training schedules which passed for education among the Spartans. Music and dancing he would learn, for both had their military uses, but reading and writing, as Plutarch remarks, 'only because they were unavoidable'. For the rest everything was designed to produce toughness, endurance and discipline, and all these of a kind which even the least sensitive champion of the English public school would hesitate to defend as likely to 'make a man of' the victim.

So schooled, at the age of twenty or thereabouts, the young man graduated to another class, that of the so-called *eirenes*, in which he remained for a part, perhaps even the whole of, his twenties, not yet a full citizen but liable for military service and for the time being occupied in doing to others as he had been done by, acting as leader of a younger group, wielding the whips rather than feeling them, and, a nice touch, allotted to one of two large teams to encourage rivalry in bravery, such rivalry that 'members of each team fall to fighting each other whenever they meet'.

At the age of thirty the Spartan was admitted to the assembly. Whether he had already received the other mark of manhood, admission to a *sussition*, either on becoming an *eiren* or on ceasing to be one, is unknown. Equally uncertain are the mechanics of admission. According to Plutarch the existing members had a right of veto on the candidate and, if each phratry had its own single *sussition*, the rejected candidate could not simply turn away and apply elsewhere—he had only one chance. On the other hand, if *kleroi* were in fact allotted at birth by the phratry authorities the potential 'Equals' were already marked out when they reached manhood, and, given that the number of *kleroi* roughly matched the desired number of 'Equals', there could be no great wastage at this stage.

At any rate, this was the last formal test the Spartan had to pass. Beyond it lay freedom, freedom to marry, to lead something like a normal life. His duties were light—he had to dine with his fellows, to train with them and to fight with them; and from his *kleros* he had to provide the stipulated contribution to maintain the mess. But it is easy to underestimate the effect even of this amount of communal living in a society where there was no other focus for a man's interests. The

Spartan did not work—he trained, with his *sussitoi*, he fought, with his *sussitoi*, or he was idle, again for the most part one would imagine with his *sussitoi*.

The Spartans boasted that they were the only soldiers in Greece who, when their line was broken, could reform and fight just as well at the side of a stranger. But this is not as one might think a mark of adaptability, far from it. It merely shows that as the individual was submerged in the little world of the *sussition*, so the *sussition* was forced into the same pattern as all other *sussitia*, identical components in a rigid military machine. As Aristotle shrewdly judged:

It is the standards of civilised men not of beasts that must be kept in mind, for it is good men not beasts who are capable of real courage. Those like the Spartans who concentrate on the one and ignore the other in their education turn men into machines and in devoting themselves to one single aspect of a city's life, end up by making them inferior even in that.

But how much of all this did Lykourgos intend? The rigid uniformity must have been imposed at some time by the state; a state magistrate, the *paidonomos*, was appointed to oversee the *agoge*, state festivals saw the performance of some of the nastier games of endurance, the *sussitia* were part of a social and military system which the state had created. All this and more can be given to Lykourgos. But he cannot have invented the institutions out of which the system was built up.

A similar *agoge* was found in Dorian Krete; so too were *sussitia* (though of a looser and more civilised kind), and, in spite of the tradition that Lykourgos made use of Kretan models, it is far more likely that both Spartan and Kretan customs were inherited from their common tribal past than that one borrowed an alien régime from the other. Indeed most Greek states preserved some vestiges of comparable habits in the easy-going but still ritually and practically important training that they gave to their young men between the ages of eighteen and twenty, while almost every aspect of the full Spartan practice can be paralleled among backward warrior tribes today. The age-groups, the communal life, the initiation ceremonies, all these had been handed down through generations as have similar institutions among the Masai in Kenya, the Zulus or the Red Indians. They were not the once for all invention of a single legislator in a comparatively civilised society.

It was Sparta's misfortune that they were formalised at a time when military efficiency was the only concern of a state education; it was Sparta's (but not Lykourgos') fault that they were then maintained, more or less unchanged, when other Greeks were discovering that there were other virtues besides the military. Aristotle was right to point out that the Spartan of his day had lost even his physical superiority, that real courage belonged to civilised men not beasts, but he was not wholly fair to Lykourgos when he concluded, 'We must judge Spartan education by the present not the past.' It was devised for a Lykourgan past, not an Aristotelian present.

Much the same is true of the third Spartan characteristic, austerity. The tradition is full of moralising stories—the ban on coinage, the simplicity of domestic architecture are only two. The Spartan youth was allowed only one cloak a year, he slept on a bed of rushes torn by his own hands from the river bank, he had to steal his food and stole it from a *sussition* where the greatest luxury was black broth—and so on. Much of this must be true and some of it must have been intended from the start, but much of it is no more than the survival of what was normal when the rules were made into a time when the good sense and the economic development of the rest of Greece were turning Greek society at large into one of the most open and flexible that has ever been known. Lykourgos himself may have worn rough clothes and washed in cold water but he would not have scorned a hot bath or a soft Milesian cloak had he known them.

Lykourgos, then, took what he found and, partly by accident, partly by design, made a system of it. He found 9,000 men who would have called themselves Spartans and he made them citizens; he found Kings, a *Gerousia* and a *demos* and he turned them into a constitutional government; he found tribes, *obai*, an *agoge* and *sussitia* and out of them made an army and a fixed way of life; he found no coins, no cakes and no Milesian cloaks, so he did not bargain for them.

This is not to say that he did not innovate. Haphazard growths do not fall into a formal place without some surgery, even if surgery is unwanted. It may be wanted and institutions can be drastically reshaped without leaving any trace on a tradition as incomplete as ours. But whatever changes, whatever new emphasis Lykourgos introduced, there is no doubt that the greatest innovation of all was the mere fact of definition, of laying down a set of rules for the first time in Sparta's history, perhaps for the first time in Greece.

(B) THE DATE OF THE REFORMS

Just how great the innovation was depends on the answer to one of the most debated problems in Greek history—the date of Lykourgos.

Greeks argued for absolute dates which in our terms work out at 1100, 1000, 885, about 810, or 776. Some modern scholars have been prepared to accept the lowest of these, others cannot imagine a defined constitution so early and on various grounds have found a plausible context around 600, others more recently have argued for a compromise around 675. What follows is only the briefest sketch of the main arguments involved.

To reject the tradition is a serious step for it is less confused than it appears. Apart from Herodotos who associated Lykourgos with King Leobotes (for him *c.* 1000 B.C.) and the Sicilian Timaios who lost heart and postulated two Lykourgoi, almost all respectable Greek historians were trying in their different ways (above p. 19 ff.) to say that Lykourgos was a contemporary of King Charillos who reigned about 776. If a *rhetra*-type constitution is conceivable in 776 we have no right to disbelieve them.

But I do not think that it is conceivable. Certainly, on my story, there was no Spartan *demos* of 9,000 to agitate for recognition nor was there land available to satisfy them before the conquest of Laconia and perhaps Messenia as well. Certainly if the *rhetra* was a written document, it did not pre-date the rediscovery of writing in Greece *c.* 750. Certainly if the Delphic oracle had any hand in blessing the new order, there was no new order before the oracle began to function seriously *c.* 750, probably not before it won international recognition *c.* 725.

And there are greater difficulties. Constitutional definition came to Athens in 594, to some other states perhaps half a century sooner. Could Sparta have been more than a century earlier still? As a result of the definition the Spartan *demos* won a kind of recognition which is startling at any time before 600 and such privileges are not usually won without a fight. Either, then, the Spartan *demos* was strong enough to fight and win, or some powerful Spartans were prepared for their own ends to encourage a *demos* which already seemed a useful ally to fight and win. In either case, where did the *demos* get its strength?

The survival of primitive communal customs might maintain a bond between ordinary Spartans which could make them more class-conscious than their fellows elsewhere; their political position too as an invading élite (for they may have thought of themselves as such) might encourage a desire for homogeneity inside the élite. But these are only arguments for setting the Spartan revolution rather earlier than those of the rest of Greece, not for raising it by more than a century. In other cities the expansion of trade and manufacture during the eighth century produced the decisive change in the basic structure of society, the economic revolution which is needed to explain the political revolutions of the seventh, the earliest of them not long before the middle of the century. The annexation of Messenia doubled Sparta's wealth at one stroke and might therefore have produced a more sudden development, earlier political consequences. But there was no comparable change in the ninth century which could produce comparable conditions in the early eighth. Then too there was political trouble, power was shifting from kings to aristocracies, but even if tensions in the higher levels of society did much to create the Spartan crisis, as they did (below p. 63) the *demos* is involved as well and a *demos* which is discontented enough to make demands, strong enough to ask for and be given recognition, is certainly unexplained and, I think, inexplicable before about 700 B.C.

Regrettably, then, the association of Lykourgos with Charillos must be abandoned, and 700 becomes the upper limit. The lower is given by a fragment of Tyrtaios which seems to paraphrase the Lykourgan *rhetra*. But when did Tyrtaios write the poem? He fought in the second Messenian War but various exact dates that are given for that war are all chronographers' calculations based on Tyrtaios' own assertion that it came two generations after the first, an assertion which must leave it floating fairly freely around the middle, preferably just before the middle of the century. A man who was fairly young in about 650 could still have been writing even as late as 600. In another fragment Tyrtaios mentions an army brigaded in its three Dorian tribes, i.e. the pre-obal army, this in a poem which probably deals with the second war. But in the vital line the verb is missing. Earlier editors restored 'We shall go into battle in tribal formation' and argued, therefore, that the changes must have followed the war. But we may just as well write 'They, *sc.* our fathers, used to go into battle . . .' and reverse the order. In yet another poem, Aristotle says, Tyrtaios spoke of political trouble in Sparta 'after the Messenian War', but did Aristotle mean the first or second war? Again Herodotos, although dating Lykourgos about 1000 B.C., seems to make his work the direct cause of Sparta's aggressive ambition which led to the Arkadian wars in the early sixth century. But even if we ignore the confusion and accept the connection, this is hardly a pointer to, say, 600 rather than 670. When did the Arkadian wars begin?

In different ways all these scraps of evidence may strengthen our confidence in seventh-century trouble and a seventh-century solution to it, but none helps to fix a precise date. It was once believed that archaeology provided one. The first interpretations of the excavations at Sparta and at the temple of Artemis Orthia presented historians with a sudden break in imports of luxury goods very soon after 600, followed by a dramatic collapse in the standard of native art. It was tempting to associate this with the imposition of a stern Lykourgan *agoge* not long before. But later reflection has shown that native art was a long time a-dying and did not even begin to wither until about 550 when the superlative inspiration of Attic black-figure pottery is quite enough to explain why Laconian potters, like others elsewhere, should lose their hearts and their markets. The magnificent bronze bowl from Vix alone is enough to prove that Laconian bronze-workers did not follow their example at once. The break in imports has also been moved down a little, to about 570, somewhat out of reach of the latest conceivable Lykourgos, and, in any case, does not demand an *agoge* to explain it. Indeed, if the archaeological evidence must be related to Lykourgos, it is much better to argue that the liberating aspect of his reforms could have helped to produce the first real flowering of Spartan art from about the middle of the seventh century onwards.

Only one argument remains. From Plutarch's *Life of Lykourgos* and some other hints it is possible to reconstruct Aristotle's story of the revolution. For him the link with King Charillos was firm but like us he was struck by the apparent paraphrase of the *rhetra* in Tyrtaios. To account for it he argued that the *rhetra* belonged to Lykourgos and the reign of Charillos but that the addition of clause V, the amendment, was the work of two later kings, Theopompos and Polydoros. His evidence for this can only have been a fragment of Tyrtaios which Plutarch quotes as if the names of the kings had actually appeared in the original poem. If they did, it is legitimate to look at the fragment again and ask if Aristotle's reasoning from it was correct, starting as he did from the false belief in an early Lykourgos. I paraphrase:

> Theopompos and Polydoros brought back from Delphi the God's oracle and decision. [For from his temple Apollo spoke in these terms]: the kings shall initiate counsel, they and the elders who watch over Sparta. And then the men of the people answering with straight *rhetrai* . . .

(I have inserted in square brackets an introductory couplet cited by Diodoros which I believe was part of the original poem. Diodoros also quotes two additional couplets at the end which add nothing of substance.)

The 'straight *rhetrai*' here must echo the 'crooked *rhetrai*' of the amendment and from this Aristotle will have persuaded himself that the kings merely reaffirmed the *rhetra* when adding the new clause. But, on the face of it, Tyrtaios was ascribing to them the introduction of the *rhetra* itself as well as the amendment, and so gives us at least a *terminus ante quem*, at best a fixed period for both. The reigns of Theopompos and Polydoros can only have overlapped between about 700 and 670.

The close association of the Karneian Games with the *agoge* might tempt one to think that they celebrated its institution—the games were reorganised in 676. This and a few other scraps of argument and evidence can be used to support a date towards the lower end of the period 700–670, most importantly that the lower it is the nearer the development of Sparta matches that of the rest of Greece, but to rehearse them would simply obscure the vital point. If Tyrtaios named the kings, he dated the revolution; if he did not, it may still belong to the same period but in honesty all we can do is let it drift where it will in the half-century or so around 650. There is no other anchor.

(c) THE CONSEQUENCES

The simple consequence of a date as early as 776 for the Spartan revolution would be such a totally new picture not only of Spartan history but of that of the rest of Greece as well that I cannot contemplate it.

The consequences of the choice between early and late seventh century are severe but supportable.

In 676 Sparta would have given a lead to the rest of Greece in recognising the enormous economic and social changes that followed the expansion of the eighth century. She would have achieved this by inventing the idea of a defined constitution, and choosing a definition which in essence was imitated by all other city-states we know of. At any time after about 650 the effects would be felt and the answer given derivatively, after others had had the same experience and given a similar answer.

Secondly, at an early date the revolution would come at the end of a period of success, before Sparta's defeat by Argos at Hysiai in 669 and the Messenian revolt. Later it comes in a period of defeat or difficulty. The distinction is of some importance for the psychology of Spartans at the time. Successful revolutions are made by men whose real power is increasing but are being barred from the recognition to which they feel entitled. In one case the barrier will be external and accidental, the Messenian revolt (compare perhaps the First World War and the Russian Revolution); in the other it will probably be no more than the persistent resistance of the established order to ever-mounting demands for change.

It is to be noted here that earlier studies of Spartan history, influenced by the belief in a sudden onset of austerity about 600, have over-emphasised the disciplinary side of the revolution, have seen it as a tightening of belts in a time of danger after the revolt. With austerity removed, more recent works have given proper weight to the liberating aspects of the changes, to the fact that any increase in discipline there may have been was a small price to pay for the new social and political equality. The former view demanded some external crisis, in the latter, popular feeling is enough.

Thirdly, at a different level, a late date demands the rejection of almost the whole Greek tradition; the earlier date does allow the retention of some elements in it, for example the story that Theopompos and Polydoros played an important part in Sparta's political development, and makes it easier to explain the aberration of the rest.

Fourthly, that the genuine figure of Lykourgos should be lost to memory needs no explanation if he was an earlier contemporary of Homer (about 776) or even a contemporary of Pheidon of Argos (about 676); it is hard to credit that the life of a man who might have talked with Periander of Korinth or Solon of Athens (about 600) should be so wholly dark. Indeed it is this darkness as much as anything that has led those who accept a late date to deny his existence. Historically the question hardly matters—the Russian Revolution would have happened and might have happened much as it did without Lenin. But Lenin, like Lykourgos, adds a touch of colour which I should be sorry to lose.

Some have explained him away as an earlier reformer who was given credit for the later constitution, others have thought of him as the god or hero under whose protection the new order was placed— by the fifth century he did receive quasi-divine honours in Sparta, something, it is said, which early Greeks did not accord to mortals. But the Spartans themselves believed that they were according these honours to a mortal and I prefer to agree with them. The narrative which follows is written on the assumption that Lykourgos was a man who did, very roughly, what the Spartans thought he did. It is written on the far more important assumption that his work can be dated to the early seventh century. It will include a few other arguments for both man and date, but neither they nor the plausibility of the story, if it is plausible, should tell more than marginally in its favour.

BIBLIOGRAPHY

See, besides the works cited in the general bibliography, H. T. Wade-Gery, *CQ*
    37 (1943) 62 ff. and *38* (1944) 1 ff. and 115 ff. (=*Essays in Greek History* (1958)
    37–85); N. G. L. Hammond, *JHS 70* (1950) 42–64; A. J. Beattie *CQ 44* (1951)
    46 ff.; A. G. Tsopanakis, *Hellenika* Suppl. iv (1954); A. Andrewes, *Probouleusis*
    (1954) and *The Greek Tyrants* (1956) ch. vi; on the working of the constitution,
    Ancient Society and Institutions (*Ehrenberg Studies*) 1 ff.; A. H. M. Jones ibid.
    165 ff.; W. G. Forrest *The Phoenix 20* (1967) 11 ff.; on the army, A. J. Toynbee,
    JHS 33 (1913) 246 ff.; on the *rhetra* as an oracle, L. H. Jeffery, *Historia 10* (1961)
    145 ff.; on the date, Forrest, *The Phoenix 17* (1963) 157 ff.; on the archaeological
    evidence, A. Blakeway, *CR* (1935) 184; J. Boardman, *BSA 58* (1963) 1 ff.;
    R. M. Cook, *CQ 12* (1962) 156 ff.; R. Joffroy, *Le Trésor de Vix* (1954); on the
    social background, W. K. Lacey, *The Family in Classical Greece* (1968), which
    appeared too late to be absorbed in the text.

5

THE REVOLUTION

Not long after the annexation of Messenia, in 708, Sparta sent out a colony to Tarentum in south Italy, her only certain colonial venture after the migration period. The motive was political trouble at home; the colonists, a dissident group called the Partheniai, 'children of unmarried mothers'. It was agreed by most respectable authorities that they were born of Spartan fathers and, apparently, Spartan mothers, but under curious circumstances which led to their not being recognised as Spartans. Disgruntled, they attempted revolution, and this sending of the colony was Sparta's solution. Details vary and the basic story has very probably been invented to explain the name, Partheniai, which might well have another, perhaps a geographical origin. Nevertheless it would seem that status had become important enough to provoke discontent which needed a drastic solution. The historian Ephoros hints at the reason: if the colony failed the Partheniai were to be given land in Messenia—surely a claim to Messenian land had lain behind the original quarrel.

The material benefits that might now be attached to 'citizenship' made it vital, as it had not been before, to define the 'citizen' and in formulating the definition the Spartans had for some reason excluded a group which was strong enough and angry enough to cause trouble. Definition is too precise a word—the process by which land or anything else was acquired will have been haphazard; but *de facto* there were now 'haves' and 'have-nots' and the 'have-nots' could not be ignored.

A crisis of this kind rarely mirrors exactly the process of which it is a part, and when revolution came to Sparta it was certainly much more complex than the Partheniai affair and indeed need not have contained any elements which directly matched it, but behind both lay the same issues, status and land, and these issues were created by the stresses put on the Spartan economy and Spartan society by the annexation of Messenia.

The economic development of other states in Greece during the eighth century brought crises there too. The aristocratic system could not adapt itself to new conditions of vastly increased and redistributed wealth or to the new sense of independence that moved down through a society which was gradually becoming familiar with the outside world. Men who had been on the fringes of power were now rich enough and confident enough to fight their way forwards and lesser men were ready to support them in exchange for privileges which we cannot always grasp in detail but, broadly speaking, added up to a recognition of their existence as citizens. The days of popular demand for direct political power still lay a century and a half ahead but the movement had begun and even in its first incoherent stages was given a weapon which made it easy to realise its demands.

This was a new army. In recent years the political consequences of the adoption in Greece of hoplite battle tactics may have been exaggerated, as has the suddenness of the adoption itself. Nevertheless, from the late eighth century onwards more and more men became rich enough to equip themselves as soldiers and an army whose effective part had once been a small group of aristocratic soloists, fighting on the Homeric pattern, began to grow into an army whose success depended on the combined efforts of a large proportion of the citizen body, heavily armoured and ranged in a solid phalanx. The aristocrat lost his military monopoly and lesser men were being brought together in an organisation which would quickly encourage the growth of class-consciousness and of class-confidence. These lesser men did not instigate revolutions—political initiative still lay with a small circle at the top—but they provided ready support for anyone who was prepared to buy political power with the concessions they wanted.

The existence of these two levels of dissatisfaction is obscured by the fact that many of the revolutions, when they came, produced a tyrant as their figurehead, in the case of Sparta by the survival of the kingship which had already given way elsewhere to pure aristocracy, still more by the fact that there were two kings who need not always have stood together. One or both might side with the existing aristocracy, with the would-be new aristocracy or might try to use the people on their own account against both, as apparently the contemporary king of Argos, Pheidon, had used his people to re establish royal authority over the nobles.

But one thing is certain. Whatever the pattern on the surface, the composition of the *Gerousia* was the issue that lay at the heart of the trouble. Its importance is insisted on by Plato and, with special reference to the *rhetra*, by Aristotle, and although the *rhetra* itself speaks only of the *Gerousia*'s size and probouleutic authority much more must have been involved, almost certainly the introduction of the system of election from a restricted noble group to replace an earlier right of membership by birth alone. If so, it is inconceivable that there were not several new faces in the first *Gerousia* so elected (or chosen by Lykourgos, if as Plutarch says he picked the first senators himself). It is inconceivable too that these new faces were not those of the men who had managed the revolution from the start. Just as each stage of American expansion towards the west threw up a new rich who became, with the next stage, a new layer of the established aristocracy, so the annexation of Messenia had upset the balance of wealth in eighth-century Sparta and now the wealthiest were winning their place in society.

But the *Gerousia* was to be elected, that is to say, the new men expected to have popular support. What price did they pay for it? Politically the price must have seemed negligible. The people were to be allowed, as they always had been allowed, to meet and express their views; they were also granted the right to meet regularly and to give or withhold a final blessing to decisions taken by the *Gerousia* after their earlier discussion. But the vital importance of these new powers might well escape their leaders—it is always easy to encourage popular authority when it is on your side, and, should the old guard ever gain a majority in the *Gerousia*, would not the people's 'final say' at the next regular assembly serve to keep it in check?

The price need not have seemed so negligible to those who were receiving it. It amounted to what was to be called 'Equality', and difficult as it is to define this equality exactly, still more to grasp the nature of the inequality which must have preceded it, it is undoubtedly a friendly word. It could have had two aspects. Lykourgos might only have been increasing the rights of an existing if ill-defined *demos* vis-à-vis the aristocracy; but he might also have been doing something to create this *demos* for the first time out of a totally disparate collection of groups or individuals, some privileged already, others such as the Partheniai had been, depressed and unrecognised. That there was an element of the second in what he did is likely enough and against such a background the word 'equality' has a much more direct and obvious content, but my inclination is to stress the other aspect to which another friendly word that was used to describe the new conditions more firmly points—*Eunomia*.

Eunomia means good order. Its opposite in early days was not an order which though orderly was bad, but simply disorder. It marked the existence of effective laws and said nothing of their quality. Comparable is the word *dike*, 'justice', again contrasted not with 'injustice' but with an absence of rules altogether, 'caprice'. These themes, order and justice, recur again and again in the revolutions that came to the Greek states in the seventh and sixth centuries and concrete embodiments of them, constitutions and law-codes, were what the successful revolutions produced. Even in a situation which we regard as the antithesis of constitutional, the setting-up of a tyranny, Kypselos the tyrant of Korinth could be praised in a contemporary source for bringing *dike* to his city. In Sparta, not long after the revolution, Tyrtaios sang the praises of *Eunomia*. Another poet, Terpander, probably in the year of the revolution itself, 676, singled out Spartan *dike* for special praise:

> The spear-points of young men blossom there . . .
> and justice is done in open air,
> the help of gallant enterprise.

In some other states inequality inside the *demos* was also an issue—Solonian Athens is an example—but in all of them the suppression or limitation of unbridled and capricious aristocratic authority was the prime ingredient, and it is not unreasonable to infer an analogous emphasis in Sparta.

Sparta will have had her own peculiar variations from the general pattern, but for them we lack evidence, as we do for the stages by which each class had reached the degree of ambition, class-consciousness or strength to exact the recognition it now won. Part of the answer lies in the no doubt tangled but unrecorded story of the first exploitation of Messenia, part of it in the similarly uncharted process by which all Greeks of the time were slowly moving from Hesiod's grumbling acquiescence in the established order to the confident assertion of individual human autonomy which was fifth-century Athens' noblest achievement. Where the average Spartan stood in 676 we do not know, but at least he was far enough advanced to act and to act a quarter of a century before his neighbours.

Curiously enough, however, he neither received nor expected any credit for this. The tradition is unanimous that Lykourgos found his laws elsewhere, according to some in Delphi, according to fifth-century Spartans in Krete. Tyrtaios is evidence that Delphi played some part, and, although the social parallels between Krete and Sparta come from a common Dorian past, the political similarities which Aristotle saw even in his own day, when the developed constitutions of both had moved well apart, could have been the result of some early borrowing. A handful of seventh-century inscriptions survive to give substance to the reputation which Kretans had as early constitution-mongers, though they give too fragmentary a picture to allow comparison with Sparta. To go further, the obvious source for Kretan ideas would be the Phoenician cities of the Syrian coast and although this is again an area where nothing is known, Aristotle also remarked on the likeness between Spartan and Kretan practices and those of Phoenician Carthage. But whatever the origin of the ideas, the application of them in Sparta was a new step for mainland Greece. What is more they were accepted without general violence at the time and administered wisely enough to save Sparta entirely from the painful squabbling that beset so many of her neighbours. True she lacked the divergent economic interests which did much to heighten tension elsewhere; true all Spartans had a common interest in preserving domestic unity against the helots; but they must also have had a certain amount of good sense.

To add personalities to such a hazy story is a risky game. But although the part played by King Theopompos is wholly obscure, something of the role and character of his colleague Polydoros may be seen. In later Sparta Polydoros had a remarkable reputation as a popular king, a distributor of land, a fair and generous judge in the courts, a reputation which sets him apart from any other Spartan king and is strikingly apt for a seventh-century reformer, so apt that I am prepared to think it genuine. If so, Polydoros, either in order to reassert royal authority against an encroaching aristocracy, or because he thought it was right, will have stood with the discontented. With his help together with that of an ambitious few and a hopeful *demos* Lykourgos dissolved the old aristocracy, created a new one which matched more closely the real power pattern, and gave to the *demos*, as Solon said of Athens, 'as much recognition as was sufficient', probably as much as it wanted. Justice, equality and order.

The last of these may seem unexciting to us; it was not unexciting then. The Greek had certain positive demands, but it was not easy even to formulate these demands without some stable background, without order; above all then he wanted to know exactly where he stood. Hence the emphasis on definition—faced with a moderately vocal *demos* Lykourgos decreed that in future it should be vocal at certain times and with certain effects, faced with tribal initiation rites and tribal education he decreed that there should be an *agoge*. Often he altered what he found and it can readily be seen why the alterations would have been welcomed (more justice, more equality), but it was the fact of a decree quite as much as the content that mattered.

There was, however, one important area where he went beyond definition but where the reasons for change are not obvious, his use of the *oba* instead of the tribe as the basis for the social and consequently the military organisation. This change, from an existing gentilicial criterion to another existing local criterion, may have been much less dramatic than has sometimes been thought, and may only have made a serious difference at the tribal/obal, not at the phratry level. But it is still a conscious change and needs an explanation. A desire for increased efficiency in training and consequently in battle, the need to recognise that local loyalty was greater than tribal loyalty as more and more ordinary men came to matter in military life, these are the only motives that occur to me—but they do not seem an entirely adequate answer.

The doubt is disturbing for the army was somewhere near the heart of the whole affair. Why else should Tyrtaios mention the change in its organisation in a poem on the Messenian revolt (above p. 56 f.)? It would seem that Spartans could be encouraged by the thought that they were no longer fighting as tribesmen but as obesmen. Indeed the fact that King Polydoros led the new army out on an aggressive campaign against Argos a year or two after the reforms (he called his son Eurykrates 'Wide-ruler', an ambitious name) could well be the result of the new army's eagerness to show off its skill. If so, like the revolutionary armies of Napoleonic France, it ventured too far and in 669 was decisively defeated by the Argives at Hysiai. As a result Argos and her Arkadian allies were able to extend their influence right across the north of the Peloponnese and take control of the Olympic festival; not only that, the new hostile belt to the north prompted Messenia to revolt.

At home the disasters brought reaction. Polydoros was assassinated by a disgruntled aristocrat and, one story has it, Lykourgos himself thought it wise to go into exile. The context suits admirably the spirit of the amendment to the *rhetra*, but not, of course, Tyrtaios' date for the amendment, which for him belonged, like the *rhetra* itself, to Theopompos and Polydoros. But there is a touch of dishonesty in Tyrtaios' paraphrase, a shift of emphasis from the authority of the *demos* to that of the kings and *Gerousia*, which betrays his politics (it may also be significant that he never mentioned Lykourgos). Could his dishonesty have gone further? Could he be trying to persuade the Spartan *demos* that the *rhetra* had been less 'democratic' than it was and that the amendment which he and his fellow reactionaries now wanted had been implicit in Apollo's original advice—'of course Apollo said that the *demos* should have the final say, but he cannot have meant the final say in producing a "crooked" decision'?

And the average Spartan accepted the implications. His confidence had been broken by the defeat at Hysiai—the result, he might be persuaded, of a 'crooked' decision—his loyalty was demanded by the threat from Messenia, and meanwhile many of his former revolutionary leaders may well have begun to find, their dignity secured, that they had more in common with the old aristocracy than with the men who had helped them into power, that they had lost the inclination to encourage popular independence.

Not that the reaction should be exaggerated. The assembly continued to play a significant part in Spartan politics and, even with the amendment added, the constitution seems to have given the ordinary man as much authority as he wanted. There is little trace of further popular agitation. Sparta had acquired what was still for its day the most advanced constitution in Greece; true it produced a closed and progressively narrowing society, but she had no need of an open one. The interests of all Spartans, rich and poor, were homogeneous and constant, and while other states acquired new interests, developed new internal tensions, made more political progress, Sparta remained static, as static as any human society can. Such ossification looks unexciting and unattractive to the outside observer, but it must be remembered that it is not necessarily unpleasant for the ossified.

BIBLIOGRAPHY

See, on the wider Greek background, A. Andrewes, *The Greek Tyrants* (1965); W. G. Forrest, *The Emergence of Greek Democracy* (1966); on hoplite warfare, A. M. Snodgrass, *Early Greek Armour and Weapons* (1964); and *JHS* 85 (1965) 110 ff.; on Kretan institutions, R. F. Willetts, *Aristocratic Society in Ancient Crete* (1955).

6

MESSENIA AND ARKADIA

The re-creation of Messenian history after 370 produced, of course, a detailed story of the great revolt, several detailed stories, out of which Pausanias has constructed the fantasy which is our one complete surviving account. There is genuine tradition somewhere behind it but so distorted by local patriotism, by the propaganda of fourth-century and later Peloponnesian states and politicians, by honest error and sheer romance, that little can be recovered.

For the date, the Tyrtaian interval of two generations between the first war and the revolt is the only firm guide. Somewhere about 660, then, and surely, therefore, a result, immediate or not long delayed, of Sparta's defeat at Hysiai in 669. All but one of the precise dates that are given stem from different calculations of the Tyrtaian gap; the exception, I suspect, is no less artificial. It comes in the form of a claim that Messenia had been enslaved for 230 years at the time of her liberation, i.e. since about 600, or rather since the reign of King Leotychidas I (230 years=7 generations). Given that Tyrtaios' war cannot be as late as Leotychidas (*c.* 625–600), that there is no other evidence for trouble in his reign but that there is evidence for a later revolt in the reign of his namesake, Leotychidas II (*c.* 490; below p. 92), the eccentric date is best explained as the result of simple confusion between the kings.

After Hysiai then, at a time when Argive influence extended right across the northern Peloponnese as far as Olympia, where she took the side of the local population of the Alpheios valley, the so-called Pisatans, in a quarrel with the dominant city of the north-west Peloponnese, Elis. The Pisatans were racially akin to their neighbours, the western Arkadians; the Eleans, like the Dorians, were newcomers from the north. One would imagine, therefore, that Argos, the Arkadian cities and the Pisatans would be likely to support the Messenians; Elis and Korinth, also threatened by Argos at the time, the Spartans. Broadly the sources agree, adding Triphylian Lepreon to Sparta and Sikyon to Messenia, but on one point they differ—Elis is allotted to the anti-Spartan coalition. Probability is against them and Elis, with Argos and Arkadia, was anti-Spartan in 370, but there is no knowing the truth.

Fourth-century politics played greater havoc with the personalities. The Messenian hero Aristomenes was no doubt a real and distinguished figure but of the characters who surround him in the story several are there only to give their fourth-century 'descendants' an Aristomenean connection. Nevertheless, two commanders of the Messenian alliance were real figures of the mid-seventh century and the myth may well be right to record their participation; these were Pantaleon, the tyrant who with his family led the Pisatan resistance to Elis and kept them independent for nearly a century, and Aristokrates, an Arkadian king either of Trapezous in the south-west or of Orchomenos in the north-east, whose grand-daughter married Periander, tyrant of Korinth (it would be pre-tyrant Korinth which supported Sparta). In the story it was the treachery of Aristokrates which led to the final Messenian defeat and, true or false, this makes it likely that the doubt about his origin arose from fourth-century dispute, for at different times both Trapezous and Orchomenos then stood apart from the rest of Arkadia. As for Aristomenes it is enough to say that although orthodoxy placed him in the seventh century one ancient author dated him to the first Messenian War, that a case can be made out for thinking that another ancient author dated him to the much later revolt of 490 and that some modern scholars are prepared to argue that this second author was right.

The war itself was neither short nor easy—so much again may be inferred from Tyrtaios—but there is a strong suggestion in the sources that it may have been fairly local, that whatever help may have come from further afield, the core of the Messenian alliance and the chief centre of conflict lay in and around northern Messenia, the area between the river Alpheios and the headwaters of the Pamisos. For this is the natural meeting place for the Messenians of Stenyklaros (Aristomenes was said to come from Andania in north Messenia), the Pisatans, Arkadians of Trapezous (if this is correct) and Spartans. And two other details fit, that the last Messenian resistance was centred on the fortress of Eira, in the hills south of the Neda valley, and that Sparta at one moment captured the Arkadian city of Phigaleia on the northern side of the same valley. This last event is not related in connection with the war but the date given to it, 659, suggests that it belongs to the same context.

We may picture, then, an attempt by the still unconquered Messenians of the upper Pamisos and the Neda, with their Arkadian neighbours, to liberate the Stenyklaros plain. They failed and at the end Stenyklaros, the southern part of the Neda valley (Phigaleia was recaptured by the Phigaleians) and probably the rest of Messenia as far as the western sea were in Spartan hands. But local or not, the war had wide implications. Behind the Messenians stood the great power of Argos, other Arkadian cities and the Pisatans. Sparta even seems to have lost the moral support of Apollo at Delphi who had blessed the *rhetra* for in the 660's the oracle praised Argos, gave advice to the Phigaleians when they lost their city, and a little later supported the installation of the tyranny in Korinth, some of whose exiled aristocrats fled to Sparta. It looks as if Sparta's moment of political reaction had lost her some influential friends without winning her any new ones.

Nevertheless she escaped further trouble. Argos became preoccupied with Korinth in the early 650's; then, probably *c.* 655, Pheidon died and Argive energy declined. Doubt about the exact dates of the Messenian war makes it uncertain whether all this helped Sparta to success in Messenia or only to security afterwards, but in the long run must explain the more or less stable peace of the next half-century. Elean pressure from the north will have done something to divert the interest of west Arkadia, while the feverish activity of the Korinthian and other tyrants around the Isthmus must have turned the eyes of north Arkadians and of Argives well away from Sparta. She herself could settle down to absorb the profits of Messenia and, at last, the fruits of her *Eunomia*.

It is not only the accidental survival of the carefree lyrics of Alkman that gives these years an air of civilised gaiety and peaceful success.

About the middle of the century Laconian potters began to follow the example of the Korinthian masters and broke away from the old and in their case not very inspired geometric standards to produce an original and, as the century went on, increasingly confident, lively and attractive style which found some favour even outside Laconia itself. In return came luxuries from abroad, from Africa, the east and Asia Minor. Foreigners too were welcomed. In the days before *Eunomia*, Herodotos says, Sparta's doors were closed to strangers, but from about 676 onwards there came a stream of foreign visitors, Terpander of Lesbos, victor at the first numbered Karneia of 676, Thaletas of Krete who may have had something to do with the introduction of another set of Games, the Gymnopaidiai in 668 (commemorating the defeat at Hysiai) and many others. And Alkman too, though he writes as a Spartan, may have had a Lydian origin.

Terpander and Tyrtaios were both poets of crisis; the one wrote of *dike*, the other of war, and already in the fragments of the second there is that emphasis on military values which became the obsession of later Sparta.

> You are the unconquered blood of Herakles.
> So be brave, fear not the number of the enemy
> Stand straight in the front rank with your shield before you
> and see your life as your enemy; the darkness of
> death should be welcome as the light of the sun.
>
> (frg. 8)

The strength of the obsession can be gauged from the treatment of Aristodemos, the sole survivor of the three hundred at Thermopylai (below p. 97). Having missed the battle through illness he was disgraced and lost his citizenship for cowardice. In telling the story Herodotos seems to echo Tyrtaios' words, though he shrinks from the doctrine as would any civilised Greek. But Alkman shows that it was not yet an obsession even in Sparta before 600. The *sussitia* may already have served their famous black broth and much-diluted wine, but although he professes a lack of interest in 'fancy food' and a liking for 'common fare, like the *demos*' there is more than a touch of the expert in his list of Laconian wines and much more feeling in his lines on 'poppy-cakes and linseed and sesame and, among the flagons, honey-cakes for boys'. For him nature made, not reeds for a soldier's bed, but flowers for a garland, and girls were girls, not battery-hens to produce Spartan warriors.

Style and subject-matter were dictated by the kind of poetry he wrote—songs for festivals. But there was a place in seventh-century Sparta for that kind of poetry and the poet himself gets the balance— 'against the steel comes the fine playing of the lyre'. A fourth-century Spartan might still have had some time for Alkman, but the steel had got the upper hand.

Alkman's delight in simple human scenes and in nature is reflected for much of the sixth century in the more and more accomplished works of the potters whose standards only begin to fail about 550; his life and vigour is there in the works of smiths and sculptors who were producing works of a high order as late as 500. And a foreign visitor could still enjoy the local wine below Taygetos. But not later than about 600 war had again become a serious business.

A grandson of Pheidon of Argos, Meltas, fought a hard war against Sparta with Arkadian allies for whom he recovered some territory. The Argives, who could not see why they should have suffered for Arkadian benefit, exiled Meltas, who fled to Arkadian Tegea. They had made a momentous mistake. Arkadia and Argos now stood each on her own and in a series of wars during the next half-century Sparta succeeded in reducing one and finally took revenge on the other for Hysiai in the Battle of the Champions in about 545.

It was a year or two before this, about 550, that Kroisos, king of Lydia, decided to make an alliance with the most powerful of the Greek states and hesitated between Athens and Sparta. Athens he found unattractive, but Sparta 'had just emerged from a very difficult period' and was now mistress of the greater part of the Peloponnese. Under her kings Leon and Agesikles (roughly 580–560) she had been generally successful in her wars but had repeatedly failed against Tegea. At one moment indeed (Herodotos does not pin the moment down but seems to imply that it was during this reign) a Spartan army had marched out to annex Tegeate territory and helotise the Tegeates, carrying with it the fetters for the job, but it was defeated and Spartans had to work the fields they had come to conquer, bound in their own chains. But in the reigns of the following kings, Ariston and Anaxandridas (from about 560), Sparta had gained the upper hand over Tegea by acquiring the bones of Menelaos' nephew and successor, Agamemnon's son Orestes, which had previously lain at Tegea. Thereafter, whenever Tegea and Sparta came to blows, Sparta triumphed.

This, from Herodotos, is the only general account of the Spartan successes which tempted Kroisos to ally with her. Its implications are that Sparta had suffered one or more defeats before 560, that she gained some signal success in the following decade, and that whatever her precise relationship with Tegea in 550 she controlled the greater part of the Peloponnese; since Argos was still untouched this should mean that Elis, some of the isthmus states and a good part of Arkadia had succumbed.

At some point, too, after 560, she had made a Spartan of Orestes (possibly of his father Agamemnon as well). Orestes himself, like his father, had two claims, a claim to rule the Peloponnese including the Argolid and a claim to the loyalty of pre-Dorians. Both of these may have been in the minds of those Spartans who first thought of annexing him for Sparta. But there was also another more specific claim. By the fifth century a part of the Orestes story was localised in the southern Arkadian plain which became the plain of Megalopolis, a plain which was the home of a local Arkadian hero, Oresthes, eponym of the small city of Oresthasion. Clearly Oresthes and Orestes had been identified and it is a reasonable guess that sixth-century Spartan propaganda made use of, if it did not originate, the identification, that is that the Megalopolis plain was the immediate prize which Sparta hoped to win.

It was an obvious prize. From the start easy communications with Messenia demanded a free passage across the southern edge of the plain and this interest had been extended by the operations of the second Messenian War which drew Sparta further west and north towards Phigaleia, involving thereby the whole area which lies south and west of the river Alpheios. The Alpheios indeed makes an admirable natural frontier for Spartan influence if not Spartan control from about 650 onwards. But the plain as a whole is a more striking geographical feature than the river which runs through it.

Herodotos, however, says nothing of Spartan ambitions in this direction. For him the plain of Tegea was the objective, probably the site of his battle of the fetters, and undoubtedly the resting-place of Orestes' bones. It too was readily accessible from Sparta by a more easterly route through Sellasia, the main road today, and a route which the Spartans are likely to have followed to meet Meltas. But Herodotos may be misleading. There is some reason to think that Tegea too may have expanded outside her own natural territory south-westwards towards the Alpheios (below p. 79), that Spartans might meet and be beaten by Tegeates at Oresthasion as well as further east. If so it is easy to see how the story was distorted, a little easier too to fit in one other probable ancient reference to the battle, a remark by Theopompos that it, or something like it, took place 'towards Orchomenos'. For Tegea's northern neighbours, Mantinea and Orchomenos, may also have extended their influence south and west across Mainalon, and the latter might have extended it so far that a Spartan move towards the north, across the Alpheios, could be seen as an advance 'towards Orchomenos'.

So we may choose to think of two Spartan setbacks before 560, one in the east at the hands of Meltas and his Argives, the other, much more serious, in or near the Megalopolis plain, serious in itself and because it would reopen at once the possibility of a link between hostile Arkadians and Messenia where resistance was not yet permanently crushed. The setbacks are not to be exaggerated—Sparta was 'successful in her other wars', whatever they may have been, and 'control over the greater part of the Peloponnese' was not won overnight. But they were severe enough to prompt a drastic revision of her policy.

Hitherto expansion had meant annexation and the acquisition of a subject population while beyond the frontier of the new territory stood a circle of hostile, fearful and provocative neighbours, always ready to take advantage of any domestic weakness. Sparta's reaction had been to attack the neighbours, to expand further, to acquire more helots, as she had tried to do in the case of Tegea. But success would have meant disaster; more helots meant more effort and yet another circle of hostility beyond the next frontier. Now this was realised and circumstances offered an answer. Argos had broken with Arkadia. If Sparta could take her place as friend of the Arkadians, she might at once win support against Argos, or at least neutrality, and rob her helots of sympathisers across the border.

Whether the seizure of Orestes' bones was intended as an announcement to the world at large that a new Sparta had been born, we do not know. Herodotos saw it as a strengthening of Spartan arms not of Spartan diplomacy and, as we have seen, it need not have been more than a propaganda blow in a local quarrel between Sparta and Tegea for Orestes' plain. On the other hand the oracle at Delphi which had links with Arkadia gave its blessing to the transfer and this reappearance of Sparta in the Delphic circle should mean some change of heart. One Spartan did feel the change strongly enough to call his son 'Philachaios' ('Friend of the pre-Dorians'). Most important of all, the superiority over Tegea which the bones had brought led not to annexation but to an alliance (below p. 79)and by the end of the century to a network of alliances which covered most of the cities of the Peloponnese. This is not to say that the Arkadians recognised or acquiesced in a change at once, if ever they did—it might well be Tegeate disapproval of Stesichoros' support for a Spartan Orestes in his *Oresteia* that led to the poet's exile from Tegea's near neighbour Pallantion. But, however obscure the mechanics, a new policy there was and Orestes became its symbol.

If so, the date is certain. Not earlier than 560, for Ariston and Anaxandridas must be on the throne; not later than about 550, for it had already taken effect when Kroisos was looking for an ally; perhaps before 553, if there is truth in the tradition that Stesichoros did not survive that year. And from the date it becomes easy to guess the architect for 556 was the year in which Chilon, wisest of all Spartans, held the office of ephor.

From this time on the college of ephors figures more and more as the most significant part of Sparta's administrative machine, largely perhaps because it is only now that there is evidence for the working of the machine but partly too because of the nature of the office. Its members (five by the late fifth century) were chosen annually by the assembly with no formal restriction on eligibility. Thus it drew its authority from a non-aristocratic source, and if there were at any time coherent opposition to a king or to the aristocracy, the ephorate would be its weapon. There was no natural opposition to either built into the office—ephors from year to year, like Roman tribunes, might be *mancipia nobilium* or *regum*—but any movement that went on beneath the surface in Spartan society, any feeling on any particular issue, could show itself most effectively through this office. That there were such movements or such feelings is shown not only by the wide judicial and executive powers which we shall see the ephors exercising within a few years of Chilon (and these must have been taken from somebody at some time) but by the fact that they later managed to replace even the kings and the *Gerousia* as presidents of the assembly.

All ancient authorities use different formulae to ascribe their origin to the neighbourhood of 700; to Lykourgos, to the reign of King Theopompos or to the year 754 which for the ancient chronographer was somewhere within Theopompos' reign. There is no comparable agreement on the original purpose of the office. Were the first ephors merely agents of the kings, as some claimed, or checks on them, as the majority thought? If *c.* 700 is the correct date for the institution it is natural to think that it was produced by the struggle between the kings and the aristocracy that is typical of the period, and there was a monthly exchange of oaths between kings and ephors that looks like the result of some early bargain—the ephors swore to support the kings, the kings swore to maintain the constitution. But it is impossible to go further without becoming involved in the unknowable complications of the Spartan crisis which we have already explored.

What matters is this. There were ephors in Sparta's first colony, Thera, traditionally founded in the generation after the Dorian invasion, in fact not later than 750. Probably then there were men in the mother city at that time who called themselves by the same name. But the name is something other than its content, and the content must have been substantially altered by formal legislation in Theopompos' reign, and again, perhaps several times, before the fifth century. Moreover there will have been other changes, many changes of emphasis and interest that needed no formal recognition. In short there is no such thing as a constant 'ephorate'; we can only contemplate the actions of this or that board or succession of boards, and, to return to the point, note that Chilon is the earliest ephor who can be credited with any solid influence. How far he shaped the office is another matter.

But solid influence he must have had—a man was not called one of the Seven Sages for nothing—and the chronological coincidence makes it easy to believe that he used it to turn Sparta from her traditional plan of conquest to the subtler and much more effective scheme that in less than half a century made her the leading power in Greece.

BIBLIOGRAPHY

See, on the Messenian tradition, F. Jacoby, Commentary on, *FGH* 265; G. L. Huxley, *Early Sparta* (1962) ch. vii; L. Pearson, *Historia 11* (1962) 397 ff.; H. T. Wade-Gery, *Ancient Society and Institutions (Ehrenberg Studies)* 289 ff. On the Pisatans, A. Andrewes, *Greek Tyrants* (1956) ch. v; on Alkman and Stesichoros, C. M. Bowra, *Greek Lyric Poetry* (2nd ed.) (1961) chs. II and III; on Tyrtaios, Bowra, *Early Greek Elegists* (1938) ch. 20; on Laconian pottery, R. M. Cook, *Greek Painted Pottery* (1954) ch. IV.5 (chronology, J. Boardman, *BSA 58* (1963) 1 ff.); on the Orestes policy, H. T. Wade-Gery, *Cambridge Ancient History* III (1925) 565 ff.; D. M. Leahy, *The Phoenix 12* (1958) 163 ff. (compare C. M. Bowra, *Greek Lyric Poetry* (2nd ed.) 112 ff.; F. Kiechle, *Lakonien und Sparta* (1963) 44 ff.); on the ephorate, the works cited in the general bibliography.

7

SPARTA AND THE TYRANTS

There is no record of how, on what terms or, precisely, when Sparta made the alliances out of which the Peloponnesian League was later constructed. But a fragment of one important record has survived; a *stele* stood on the banks of the Alpheios advertising a Tegeate promise to Sparta 'to expel all Messenians . . . and not to make them citizens of Tegea'. The placing of the stone supports the suggestion that the river served as the frontier between Tegea and Sparta, the provision confirms that security in Messenia had been one of Sparta's chief motives in seeking agreement (and hints perhaps at recent trouble in Messenia). Sparta's second aim, to gain a free hand against Argos, was also achieved. In 546 Kroisos sought his ally's help against the Persians but Sparta could do nothing because she was engaged in a war against Argos for possession of Thyreatis, north-west of Sparta between Arkadia and the coast, the area she had coveted and failed to win at Hysiai. Three hundred champions from either side fought in a formal contest and for the most part died trying to reach an acceptable decision, but the rules had not been properly agreed and a full-scale battle was needed in the end. Its outcome was clear, the Thyreatis became Spartan and with it the whole coastal strip down to Cape Malea and the island of Kythera. No mention is made of Arkadia in this campaign as ally of either side, and that, one might guess, was a solid gain for Sparta due to Orestes.

But for Sparta's reputation in the centuries that followed, the years after 556 were not a period of domestic consolidation or of expansion at the expense of Argos, they were the period when Sparta 'put down the tyrants'. The fact was known to Herodotos, for a long list we have to turn to Plutarch: the Kypselids in Korinth and Ambrakia, Lygdamis in Naxos, Hippias in Athens, Aischines in Sikyon, and other names which take us on to the time of the Persian Wars. And one source links Chilon with the process. That Sparta should have been active in Korinth as early as 582 (when the tyranny fell) is almost unthinkable and an attractive emendation would produce Kerinthos, a small Euboian city which had Kypselid connections. If it is accepted, action there as in Ambrakia is likely to be early rather than late in the series but is not precisely datable; nor is the success against Lygdamis (525 when Sparta took unsuccessful action against another Aegean tyrant, Polykrates of Samos, is a possible context, so is 515); Hippias was expelled in 510 but for Aischines there is doubt again—either 556 or *c.* 510 is possible, with the balance slightly in favour of 556.

Given these chronological doubts it is pointless to attempt a continuous story, but it is tempting to look for some general explanation of such a general phenomenon. Few will see a wholly adequate one in a genuine hatred of tyranny as such. Hatred of tyranny could be felt in the sixth century (witness the poems of Solon) and many Spartans may have felt it, but not strongly enough to prevent their government from trying to establish a new tyrant in Athens soon after the expulsion of Hippias, or a year or two later from trying to restore Hippias himself.

There must be, then, some more practical motive and one might be provided by the rising threat of Persia in the east. It was against Persia that Kroisos had sought Spartan help in the first place and when his capital fell to Kyros about 545 so that the Greek cities of the Ionian coast were threatened, the Spartans sent an embassy across the Aegean to 'warn' the Great King that they would not allow Greeks to become his subjects. Thereafter the attack on Polykrates was mounted just after he had shown his submission to Persia by sending help to Kambyses for the Egyptian campaign of 525; Hippias was expelled shortly after he had contracted a marriage alliance with the pro-Persian tyrant of Lampsakos, and further intervention in Athens came hard on the heels of Athenian negotiations with the Persians; while, to look ahead, in 491 Spartans did their best to neutralise Aigina when she gave in to Persia and in the end it was Sparta who led the resistance to Xerxes' invasion of 480.

On the other hand, whenever Sparta was invited to intervene directly against Persia she refused—no help was sent to Kroisos, to the Ionians when they were subdued, to Polykrates' successor Maiandrios when about 516 he came to Sparta for help, to the Skythians when about 513 they proposed a joint expedition, to the Ionians in their great revolt of 499, or even to the Athenians when in 490 Persian forces landed in mainland Greece at Marathon. There may have been good reasons on each occasion for Spartan inaction, but it is very persistent inaction. When it is added that Sparta proposed to restore Hippias when he already had links with Persia, that throughout the period she was close to the Delphic Oracle which showed signs of collaboration with Persia as early as 540 and went on to take a completely defeatist line in 480, it becomes hard to believe that fear of Persia was the main factor in Spartan thinking, at any rate before Persia posed a real threat to Greece, a threat which the perceptive might have sensed in 514 (when Skythia was invaded) but few can have felt deeply before Ionia was crushed in 494.

This is not to deny Sparta any interest whatsoever in the world outside the Peloponnese. Her alliance with Korinth would involve her in Korinth's wide interests overseas—hence no doubt her share in reducing what remained of the former tyrant-family's empire in Ambrakia and perhaps Kerinthos. And she had interests of her own. Thera's colony Kyrene in north Africa had ties of trade as well as blood with her grandmother city; Samos, also linked with Kyrene, has produced larger quantities of imported Laconian pottery than any other site. In other words Sparta had a place in Mediterranean and Aegean politics and, although this makes it more likely that she should be conscious of and react to Persia, it also makes it reasonable to look to the Aegean itself for a more immediate explanation of her activity; to the Aegean ultimately, but first even closer at hand.

One reason for the Spartan attack on Hippias in 510 was, according to Aristotle, the tyrant's friendship with Argos. An early mark of this friendship had been the marriage of Peisistratos, Hippias' father, to an Argive noblewoman who had previously been, a nice coincidence, wife of a Kypselid of Ambrakia. Peisistratos also had very close ties with Lygdamis of Naxos and there is some evidence of a further link between Lygdamis and Polykrates. Peisistratos and Polykrates, perhaps Lygdamis too, were also united by a common interest in Delos, the Aegean cult-centre of Apollo; the Peisistratids, Polykrates and the later Kypselids all shared the enmity of Sparta's friend, the Apolline oracle at Delphi.

There are signs, then, faint ones it must be admitted, of some sort of association between all but one of the powers whom Sparta chose to attack during these years. It would be wrong to picture two firm rival blocs, the one Spartan-dominated, the other Argive-inclined, persisting throughout the second half of the century as an unchanging background to Spartan foreign policy—Polykrates' *volte-face* on the Persian question, for example, must have had repercussions throughout the Aegean— but even the loosest of groupings, so long as Argos is included in it, offers a better explanation of Sparta's actions than dedication to an ideal or fear of the barbarian.

Orestes had given her security at home and a claim to Arkadia. In pursuing the claim she might well have been drawn into action in Sikyon (if the deposition of the tyrant there is properly dated to 556), for Sikyon too had very close ties with Arkadia. Perhaps at the same time she could have made an alliance with Sikyon's neighbour Korinth. So, with some powerful friends and a docile Arkadia she could turn her attention to Argos and to associates of Argos further afield. Still further away was Lydia, a Lydia possessed of strange ideas for distant conquests in the east but sufficiently involved in Aegean affairs to seem an attractive ally for more local purposes. The loss of Lydia was a serious blow but even without her help the purposes were achieved; Argos was beaten, the Peloponnese secured, and as the leading military power in Greece Sparta could help her friends and harm her enemies much as she chose. Some of those enemies were tyrants, some were friends of Persia and the fact that they were might increase her enmity. I doubt if it ever provoked it in the first place.

Orestes, then, had worked wonders, but not everyone in Sparta had approved of his adoption. About 545 the Agiad king Anaxandridas had been on the throne for some fifteen years but was still childless. Concerned for the succession the ephors of the year summoned him to them (it is a signal mark of the office's authority that a king was obliged to obey their summons at the third time of asking) and recommended divorce. Anaxandridas, who loved his wife, refused and consequently the ephors, together now with the *Gerousia*, proposed that he should break with custom and marry a second wife without divorcing the first. The king gave way to the threats which accompanied the suggestion and married again—so much had the Lykourgan system by making the monarchy constitutional reduced its powers (later theorists did not dream up the theory of a mixed constitution out of nothing).

The second wife produced a child, the later king Kleomenes, but Anaxandridas at once restored his attention to the first who herself, to everyone's astonishment, gave birth in immediate succession to three sons, Dorieus, Leonidas and Kleombrotos, the last two perhaps as twins. Thus far Anaxandridas is no more than a temporarily unhappy victim of circumstances, but the name of one son and the identity of the second wife give the whole affair more significance and more poignancy.

In the atmosphere of the mid-century the naming of Dorieus ('the Dorian') cannot be accidental—it shouts out Anaxandridas' hostility to Chilon's policy. The second wife came from Chilon's family. Perhaps the affront to royal independence created the hostility, perhaps the hostility was already there and the affront was calculated to bring the Agiad house into line; either way there was a struggle for power somewhere behind the Philachaian façade of Sparta, and one of the casualties was the child Kleomenes. Unwanted by his father, all the more when Dorieus was born, brought up in Chilon's shadow as a future agent of the Chilonian policy which his father publicly rejected, he found the strain too great—according to Herodotos he was from the start 'not in full control of himself and on the verge of madness'. And yet in most modern histories he is a great, if not the greatest of Spartan statesmen. That he was energetic, ruthless, ingenious, ambitious for himself and for Sparta, all this cannot be doubted; but to judge by the results, there is little to be said for his foresight, his wisdom or his greatness. Greece was stronger at the end of his reign than at the beginning, strong enough and united enough to defeat Persia in 480, but she was stronger because Sparta was comparatively weaker, and this weakening was largely Kleomenes' doing.

BIBLIOGRAPHY

See, on the Tegea alliance, F. Jacoby, *CQ 38* (1944) 15; D. M. Leahy, *The Phoenix 12* (1958) 163 ff.; W. K. Pritchett, *Studies in Ancient Greek Topography* (1965) 122 ff.; H. T. Wade-Gery, *Ancient Society and Institutions (Ehrenberg Studies)* 297 ff.; on the tyrants, D. M. Leahy, *Chilon and Aeschines* (1956) and M. E. White, *The Phoenix 12* (1958) 2 ff.

8

THE REIGN OF KLEOMENES

Kleomenes came to the throne sometime between 520 and 516. Thucydides places in 519 an alliance between Athens and the small Boiotian city of Plataia, an alliance proposed by Kleomenes as king, in the hope, it was said, that he might cause trouble between Athens and Boiotia's leading city, Thebes. But there are arguments, though not compelling ones, for changing Thucydides' text to produce 509. If we do, the first recorded event of the reign becomes an admirably incorruptible resistance to attempted bribery by a refugee from Persian-dominated Samos, Polykrates' successor Maiandrios, seeking no doubt a repetition of the earlier Spartan expedition. Kleomenes instructed the ephors to see that he left Sparta, this in about 516.

His accession at once produced an open quarrel between the two branches of the Agiad line. From the start Chilon's family had feared for Kleomenes' claim to the throne (they had insisted on an official inspection of Dorieus' birth) and with reason, for Dorieus grew up to challenge the claim and such was his resentment when Kleomenes as first born was preferred that he chose to leave Sparta and found a colony in north Africa. The colonists left, without the normal consultation of Chilon-tainted Delphi, without, Herodotos adds, any of the usual formalities, and settled at Kinyps in Libya, apparently a purely private venture provoked by personal pique. More may in fact have been involved, the Spartan authorities may have been able somehow to turn Dorieus' anger to their own purposes (Spartan interest in north

Africa has already been noted), but if so nothing can now be seen of what they wanted.

One certainty was that any interference in the area which Dorieus chose would invite Carthaginian hostility and two years after his arrival Dorieus was driven out of Africa and returned to the Peloponnese. But he was soon prompted to another anti-Carthaginian adventure, this time in western Sicily. Now he did take the precaution of consulting Delphi, which may imply a change of heart either at Delphi or in Dorieus, but with no greater success; the adventure led him into further complications of western Greek politics, and out of Spartan history and life.

Dorieus was probably accompanied on his last expedition by some people of Anthana, a perioikic city of Thyreatis, whose eponymous hero Anthes is linked with Kleomenes in a curious little story. Kleomenes, it runs, flayed Anthes and wrote oracles on his skin. Through the legend there might be a glimpse of further opposition between the half-brothers; there is also in the mention of oracles our first glimpse of one of the most striking features of Kleomenes' career, his remarkable and remarkably ambivalent attitude towards the gods; no one used or abused religion so much as he.

Most Greeks indeed believed that it was for sacrilege that he was punished by his madness. The Spartans disagreed—his brain had been turned by drinking wine unmixed with water, a habit he had learned from Skythian ambassadors who came to propose a joint invasion of Asia Minor after the misguided Persian expedition against them in 514. Their plan was rejected but the habit stuck.

It must have been about the same time as the Skythian embassy that Sparta began to plan for the expulsion of the Peisistratid tyrant from Athens. A leading Athenian family, the Alkmeonids, in exile at Delphi, persuaded the oracle to win Spartan support for their return. It is unlikely that the Spartans needed much encouragement, for Hippias' brother had been assassinated in 514 and in the unrest which followed the murder Sparta must have seen an easy chance to dispose of yet another friend of Argos. A naval expedition failed but in 510 the Spartan army advanced by land into Attika, besieged Hippias and his friends on the Akropolis and, when chance put the children of the family in its hands, forced him to leave the country.

This first major Spartan adventure in mainland Greece north of the

Isthmus was commanded by Kleomenes, but any part he played in the planning of it is not recorded, nor is anything known of the arrangements he may have made for the government of Athens after he withdrew. But two years later he had to return. Rivalry between the Alkmeonid Kleisthenes and another aristocrat, Isagoras, led the former into dangerous popular ways and Isagoras called on Kleomenes for help. A diplomatic *démarche* was enough—Kleisthenes and his family left the country, but Kleomenes decided to make sure; he arrived in Athens with a small force, expelled 700 more families and then tried to confirm Isagoras' authority by revising the constitution. This was too much for the Athenians who besieged Kleomenes in the Akropolis as he had besieged Hippias, quickly forced him to surrender and quit Attika.

Thus far only Kleomenes' personal interest was involved (rumour was that the interest centred on Isagoras' wife) but now he had to call for the backing of the Spartan assembly. An army of Spartans and their allies was assembled for an invasion of Attika and this could not be done by the kings alone. True, Herodotos says that they had such a right and that the purpose of the expedition was concealed by Kleomenes but this must mean the precise purpose, to instal Isagoras in power as a tyrant, not the general aim of punishing the Athenians for the affront.

In the event this secretiveness was disastrous, for neither Sparta's other king, now Demaratos son of Ariston, nor all of Sparta's allies had any stomach for such a high-handed scheme. Once in Attika the Korinthian contingent decided to abandon the enterprise, the two kings quarrelled, Demaratos refused to go further and, followed by other allies, went home. Moreover the expedition's collapse allowed the Athenians another startling success. Somehow Kleomenes had persuaded the Boiotians to concentrate their anger on Athens rather than on the real author of the Plataian alliance and, with the Chalkidians of Euboia, they had been ravaging the northern frontier of Attika while the Peloponnesians were squabbling in the west. Now the Athenians marched against them and routed both armies on the same day.

Sparta's credit cannot have stood high in central Greece, nor in the Peloponnese. When next we hear of a Spartan proposal for joint action with her allies there is no question of the king leading out an expedition ignorant of its purpose. There is a meeting of delegates, a debate and in effect a vote, the first hint that the Spartan alliance had become a League.

A primitive alliance is an agreement between two states here and now to attack a third party or to defend each other against an attack. As such it raises no problems. But as soon as it becomes a little more sophisticated, a general agreement to attack or defend each other against any third party who may arise, an essential question has to be settled—who shall say who is to be attacked and when? At one extreme either contracting party can be defined as *arbiter foederis*, an arrangement which Greeks would still call alliance (*symmachia*) but which clearly marks out one ally as master; at the other, Greeks devised a new diplomatic formula, what we would call a defensive alliance, an *epimachia*, in which, obviously, the attacker took the decision; in between no definition was attempted, each party swore to 'have the same friends and enemies' and it could be left to either to invoke the treaty, as Kroisos thought he could when he summoned the Spartans to join him in his projected attack on Persia.

Later on Sparta would impose on newly-acquired members of her League an unequal treaty of the first type by adding a clause which bound them to 'follow wherever the Spartans might lead', but there is no evidence for sixth-century procedure apart from Herodotos' vague remark—'the greater part of the Peloponnese was *under her control*'. This certainly suggests an element of inequality, but such things do not demand formal acknowledgement.

The doubt is important. When the Korinthians abandoned the campaign against Athens, were they breaking their treaty or were they merely disagreeing about whether Athens should be regarded as their friend or Sparta's enemy? In either case the creation of a League assembly whose decisions were binding on Sparta as on all other members, although strengthening the alliance in the long run, was a severe blow to Spartan prestige and power, but in the former it will have been underlined by Sparta's formal admission that she could no longer command obedience, that her hegemony had become in theory purely executive.

The set-back may have been disguised. After the kings' quarrel a law was passed that in future only one king should command an expedition. The obvious motive would be to avoid further humiliating disagreements in the field, but the measure may have been more subtle. If the original treaties had contained a promise to follow wherever, not the Spartans, but the kings might lead, to keep one king at home would automatically free the ally from his obligation (below p. 91) and the clause would not have to be withdrawn. But that is speculation; disguisedly or not, Sparta had climbed down.

But the feud with Athens was not given up. Urged on, one suspects by Kleomenes, certainly by oracles which Kleomenes claimed that he had found on the Athenian Akropolis (religion again), the Spartans summoned a congress of the League and proposed that they should restore the ex-tyrant Hippias. To explain this astonishing suggestion they argued that Hippias had always been their friend, that their action against him had been, they thought, a pious duty laid upon them by the god of Delphi whose servants, they now 'discovered', had been bribed by the Alkmeonids. Not surprisingly they did not persuade a majority of the allies. Led once more by the Korinthians the congress rejected the plan and Hippias, who had come hopefully from Asia for the meeting, withdrew to a more sympathetic Persian court.

This must have been about 503 B.C. Kleomenes is next heard of in 499. In the first moments of the Ionian revolt against Persia the Ionian leader, Aristagoras, came to Greece in search of allies, and Kleomenes, with an incorruptibility which this time had to be prompted by his eight-year-old daughter, Gorgo, ordered him from Sparta. In view of the failure of the revolt it is easy to commend Kleomenes for his prudence and to blame the Athenians who did offer brief support; but it is also easy to overdo the praise or blame, particularly if we think of the whole affair as an attempt by one small province to take on the whole might of Persia. It was much more a struggle inside the empire between Greeks who looked for some kind of autonomous existence under indirect Persian control and the local Persian governor and his friends, both parties equally intriguing for the Great King's favour. As such it was not utter folly; indeed even on the former view it is to be remembered that these same Ionians, with Athenian help, did keep the Persians out of the Aegean for about seventy years after 480.

Be that as it may, Kleomenes would have none of it; his ambitions were fastened on nearer objectives. He had unintentionally built up the strength and won the hatred of Athens but he still had Boiotian sympathy and, therefore, some link with Aigina (which had helped

Boiotia against Athens) and at some point before 500 he had reached an understanding with the leading family of Thessaly, the Aleuadai, the family which later led Thessaly into Medism. (It is remarkable how many of Kleomenes' associates of these years, Boiotia, Aigina, Delphi, Thessaly, appeared on the Persian side, if, as has been claimed for Kleomenes as for Sparta, he was already trying to rally Greece against a possible invasion.)

This was no mean alliance and about 494 he set out to strengthen it still further by humbling the old enemy, Argos. With some, perhaps unwilling, help from Aigina and Sikyon, he ferried his army across the Gulf of Argos from Thyrea and contrived to rout the Argive army at Sepeia—having accustomed the Argive army to Spartan routine he opened the attack when the call for breakfast was sounded. He then massacred the bulk of the survivors by firing a sacred wood in which they had taken refuge. Argive power was thus crushed for a generation, but, strangely, Kleomenes made no attempt on the city itself, perhaps with the intention of repeating his Athenian experiment of installing a puppet government.

If so, the experiment failed again, not for Kleomenes who was dead before he needed to call on the new Argos for help, but for Sparta—Argos took Persia's side in 480. It also failed if he hoped to find wholehearted approval at home. On his return he was prosecuted for not pursuing his success and, though he was acquitted by the ephors in whose court he was tried, even an unsuccessful prosecution cannot but dim the victor's glory.

The charge was bribery, the defence religion, the former normal for Greece, the latter normal for Kleomenes—an oracle which forecast the capture of Argos had been fulfilled when he burned the sacred wood which, as luck would have it, was called the grove of Argos. It was again corruption and religion that figured a little later behind his final coup.

The collapse of the Ionian revolt in 494 opened the way for Persian advance in mainland Greece. Athens, after years of dithering, decided for resistance, and Kleomenes too, having faced the Persian issue (I would guess for the first time), reached the same answer. Persian envoys who came to Athens and Sparta demanding submission were put to death. But those who went to Aigina were welcomed and so, with positions reversed, Kleomenes found himself a friend of Athens against

Aiginetan medism. Crossing to Aigina he demanded hostages for their good behaviour; the Aiginetans refused to obey one king without his colleague (they had probably joined the League after Sepeia and may now have been appealing to the interpretation of the two-kings law suggested above, p. 89), knowing that Demaratos would not support Kleomenes' demand. But Kleomenes, who was not a man to take defeat lightly, arranged that Demaratos' right to the throne should be challenged on the ground that he was not Ariston's son and made sure that Delphi, when consulted by the worried Spartans, would support the challenge. Demaratos was deposed (later he fled to Persia) and was succeeded by his cousin Leotychidas II whose favour Kleomenes had already won. The hostages were taken.

But yet again the success was hollow. The truth leaked out and Kleomenes fled from Sparta in a panic, first to his friends in Thessaly, then back to the Peloponnese, to Arkadia where he worked on Arkadian hatred of Sparta to produce a pan-Arkadian alliance (about this time the majority of Arkadian cities came together in a League of their own; if Kleomenes did not create it he certainly gave it an immediate objective—'against Sparta'). But this too came to nothing. The frightened Spartans invited Kleomenes home and, deserting his Arkadians, he returned, only to be struck at once, Herodotos says, with open madness—he took to beating any Spartan that he met about the head. Even the Spartans found this extension of their youthful habits irksome and the madman was put in chains where at last he committed suicide by a nasty process of self-mutilation.

The story would gain in depth if we knew more of the context. According to Herodotos the Persian envoys came in 491 but the deposition of Demaratos, the death of Kleomenes and its consequences, an attempt to recover the Aiginetan hostages from Athens, a war between Athens and Aigina, are over before the Persian fleet sets out for Greece in 490. The compression is too great; either the Athenian triumph against the Persians at Marathon should be placed somewhere in the middle of the story or the upper limit of Herodotos' account must be ignored and Kleomenes' Aiginetan adventure dated to 493 or 492. In any case two vital points in Spartan history remain unattached to the Kleomenes saga, the failure to appear at Marathon when their new allies really needed help (even if the religious obstruction which they pleaded was genuine, it was an excuse rather than a reason), and an obscure but real helot revolt of about this time, perhaps serious, perhaps not, which is not mentioned by Herodotos but for which the cumulative evidence, literary and archaeological, is strong.

As things are we can only say that Kleomenes' final endeavours probably helped to keep Aigina neutral and perhaps helped to stiffen Athenian resistance to the invasion, but they damaged Sparta's hold over Arkadia and must have helped to loosen her hold over the helots and discourage active support for Athens.

But if these are the facts of Kleomenes' career, so far as we know them, does any pattern appear? The answer, I think, is yes. On his seizure of the Athenian Akropolis in 508 the priestess tried to exclude him, as a Dorian, from Athena's temple. 'I am no Dorian but an Achaian', Kleomenes replied, surely a declaration of support for the Orestes policy. Other details fit; like Chilon Kleomenes had Arkadian connections, like Chilon he was close to Delphi, like Chilon he seems to have believed in expansion by alliance rather than subjection (at Athens and again perhaps in Argos). There is a case then for saying that he learned his lessons at his mother's knee and went on trying to apply them to the end. But if political greatness demands firmness of principle, it also demands flexibility in application and of this Kleomenes shows no sign. Spartan politicians of 520–490 had to face two great problems which Chilon could not have foreseen, the extension of Spartan influence outside the Peloponnese and the appearance of Persia. There is no hint that Kleomenes recognised the existence of the second before his intervention in Aigina in, say, 491, and in the confused and unsuccessful intrigues of 519 to 503 no trace of a real appreciation of the difficulties raised by the former.

This is not to say that there was an easy answer; far from it. Aigina was close to Argos; Korinth had interests which clashed with those of Aigina; so had Athens, but among Athenians the Alkmeonids had Aiginetan friends; to include the Thebans and Thessalians in the calculations meant further complications and contradictions. But if there was no answer, a wise man would not have interfered, at least not quite so recklessly; if there was an answer, a great statesman should have got it. Kleomenes did not; he meddled and failed.

And thanks to this meddling even Sparta's Peloponnesian authority was threatened. Her most powerful international ally, Korinth, was temporarily estranged; her most powerful local ally, Arkadia, was united against Sparta so effectively that it took more than twenty years to re-establish a proper relationship; all her allies together imposed on her the acceptance of a League constitution which for all its long-term benefits was an immediate check; when the Persians landed for the first time in 490 there was no Peloponnesian to meet them, and when they came again in 480 the Greek states, which united under Sparta's nominal command, owed their deliverance in the end not only to Sparta but even more to an Athens which Kleomenes had created but had created by mistake and had done his best to destroy.

But mad or bad? All Greeks agreed on madness, the Spartans explaining it by his drinking habits, others by his sacrilege against the sacred grove of Argos, against Delphi by the corruption of 491, against Demeter at Eleusis whom he trespassed against in 506; but madness is common to all, and a recent psychological study has pointed out that the details of his final self-mutilation are in fact consistent with a paranoid schizophrenic suicide; moreover both the inconsistency he showed towards religion and his rigid application of inherited principles, unadapted to changing circumstances, are equally characteristic of this condition, a condition that can for long be combined with an apparent near-normality, even cleverness, revealing itself only in a degree of violence, ruthlessness and an inability to get on with people (Kleomenes provides illustrations of all three in plenty).

Madness, then, and suicide, or a career of genius cut short perhaps by murder, arranged and hushed up by the Spartan authorities. I am inclined to agree with the Greeks, Argives, Athenians, Spartans and others as Herodotos reports them—Kleomenes was never wholly balanced and in the end broke down completely when the strain became too great. It is even possible that sacrilege was in a sense the cause, for around 500 B.C. Greeks still believed in their gods and so no doubt did Kleomenes. His ambivalent attitude might be a mark of light-hearted cynicism when we see it in a Cicero; it could be a heavy burden for a sixth-century Greek to carry.

BIBLIOGRAPHY

On Kleomenes see the works cited in the general bibliography, especially G. L. Huxley, and J. Wells, *Studies in Herodotus* (1923) ch. 4; I hope to publish shortly, with G. Devereux, the arguments for Kleomenes' madness; on Dorieus, T. J. Dunbabin, *The Western Greeks* (1948) ch. xi; A. von Stauffenberg, *Historia 9* (1960) 180–215; on the Peloponnesian League, J. A. O. Larsen, *CP 28* (1933) 257 ff. and *29* (1934) 1 ff.; on Arkadia, W. P. Wallace, *JHS 74* (1954) 32–5; A. Andrewes, *The Phoenix 6* (1952) 1 ff.; on the Helot Revolt see bibliography to ch. vi (under 'Messenian tradition').

9

THE PERSIAN WARS AND AFTER

The decade after the death of Kleomenes is an empty one. The helot revolt was tidied up not later than 488 and helot refugees were found a home in Sicilian Zankle by Anaxilas of Rhegion; somehow or other relations with Arkadia were patched up though not properly repaired; Athens and Aigina fought each other or thought of fighting each other intermittently without, it seems, any further fear of Spartan intervention. At home the thrones were held by Leotychidas and by Leonidas, half-brother and son-in-law of Kleomenes, and, so far as we know, all was peaceful; meanwhile the former Eurypontid king, Demaratos, was at the Persian court.

And it was the exile who produced the most moving and the best assessment of Sparta's contribution to the Greek victory of 480 and 479, an assessment, too, which cannot but do something to modify one's natural distaste for Sparta and its generally so unattractive citizens:

Want has always been our neighbour in Greece but we have courage as an ally, a courage fashioned out of wisdom and firm laws. With its help we fight off both want and slavery. . . . When the Spartans fight singly they are as brave as any men, but when they fight together they are supreme among all. For though they are free men, they are not free in all respects; law is the master whom they fear, far more than your subjects fear you [Xerxes]. They do what the law commands and its command is always the same, not to flee in battle whatever the number of the enemy, but to stand and win, or die.

There is more than a touch of romance here; Spartans surrendered to the Tegeates about 560 and to the Athenians in 425 like any troops when the case is hopeless. And the war against Persia had its moments of selfishness, error and muddle like any other war. But this was a battle against such odds that the heroism hides the faults and it has never been shown at a moment when it mattered more for what we now call civilisation. Sometimes the Spartans had to be pushed into showing it, sometimes they stumbled into showing it, but show it they did.

Of the diplomatic preliminaries little is known, even less of the part Sparta played in them. In 481, when invasion was already imminent, a Congress was summoned of all the Greek states who were ready to resist. Representatives met at the Isthmus of Korinth, Sparta was chosen as the leader of the resistance, internal squabbles were settled, chiefly that between Athens and Aigina, envoys were sent, sensibly but fruitlessly, to beg for help elsewhere, in Syracuse, Kerkyra, Krete and Argos, and the first preparations for defence were made. That Sparta should emerge as the automatic choice as leader is no surprise—whatever the constitution that this new League of the Greeks was given, it was in effect no more than an extended Peloponnesian League; Athens was the only major power to appear which was not already a member. But the fact that Sparta chose to take an interest at all has not, perhaps, been sufficiently noted. If, as I believe, she was not concerned with the Persian threat before about 493 she could well have argued, however short-sightedly, that Persian action had been prompted by Athenian stupidity, that Athens should take the consequences, that Persian interest could be stopped at the Isthmus. After the insults she had received north of the Isthmus in the previous thirty years it would have been easy for her to refuse responsibility. Instead she took the lead and in doing so showed that she understood the threat and that when her freedom was at stake the Tyrtaian 'virtues' of stubbornness, courage and obedience could take on a noble colour.

The military problem posed by the pattern of the Persian invasion was a simple one, to find a spot or spots where the Greek fleet and Greek army, severally or together, could hold the numerically much superior Persian fleet and army and allow neither to help the other; and to inflict such a defeat, negative or positive, on the invaders that they would withdraw. The obvious answer was to stand at the Isthmus and in the Saronic Gulf. But there was a much less simple diplomatic problem, to retain the loyalty of all the states who had decided to fight, perhaps even to win some who wavered. It might be argued that most of those north of the Isthmus were committed to Persia or were so uncertain or so unimportant that they did not deserve the trouble or the risk. But there was one obvious exception, Athens, who provided the bulk of the fleet without which any resistance at all would be pointless.

Hence the decisions taken by the Congress which met again in spring 480, a scheme, soon abandoned, to defend the approach to Thessaly at Tempe, and the unhappy if glorious attempt to hold the pass at Thermopylai and the strait at Artemision. But despite their failure, neither of these plans was stupid in conception or seriously damaging in the event—and there were good diplomatic reasons for both, the chance of gaining Thessalian support by the first, the absolute need to make some show of defending Attika and other northern loyalists by the second. In each Sparta played her part, so far as we know, willingly. A Spartan general, not a king, led an allied force of 10,000 hoplites north to Tempe, and quickly and wisely back again; a Spartan admiral commanded the Greek fleet, including ten ships from Laconia, at Artemision; and Leonidas himself marched out to hold Thermopylai with about 7,000 hoplites, 4,000 of them from the Peloponnese, 300 from Sparta. Some have seen culpable Spartan reluctance in the small size of Leonidas' force and in the failure to send him reinforcements, but the decision was probably wise. Only if Thermopylai and the sea beside it could be held would more troops be needed, to block other routes and relieve the victors. And it was lost through the incompetence of an allied contingent, not through weakness.

But reluctant Sparta certainly became when her 300 men and her king were killed, and she remained reluctant even when the Athenian-inspired victory at Salamis sent the Persian fleet and much of the Persian army back to Asia. The fleet she commanded hesitated to pursue the retreating Persians in 480, and her army did nothing to prevent a second occupation of Attika in 479. Sparta would not move her land forces outside the wall which was quickly thrown across the Isthmus until tough Athenian pressure, not to say blackmail, forced her to lead the allied army into central Greece for the final destruction of the remaining Persians at Plataia. But here too, selfish though her behaviour was, it was militarily defensible. The Peloponnese itself was not secure; Argos was not likely to let loyalty to Greece rob her of a chance to cause trouble, contingents from Elis and Arkadian Mantinea were suspiciously late for Plataia and other Arkadians did not turn up at all. Besides, the Persians in Greece were still as strong as any army the Greeks could put into the field; left alone they might withdraw, might be compelled to withdraw by Greek naval success in the Aegean; engaged they might win, and Greek morale might not have survived defeat.

Spartan strategy, then, was cautious, defensive, but reasonable; Spartan generals in the field, with the possible exception of Leonidas, did not show much skill in executing it. Eurybiadas, the admiral of 480 (the Spartans rarely sent their kings to sea), scarcely appears in the confused story of Artemision but at Salamis he showed neither good sense nor authority. He it was who took the decision to fight, but the idea came from an Athenian and Eurybiadas accepted it with his thoughts focussed far more on the Isthmus behind him than on the tactical opportunities of the strait of Salamis, and he followed up the victory with little more enthusiasm than his brothers on land. So long as the Persians were moving in the right direction he was happy. His successor for the campaign of 479, King Leotychidas, showed no greater verve or foresight. Under his command the next success was won at Mykale in Asia Minor but his only reaction to victory was to propose an immediate withdrawal and the transplanting of the liberated Ionian Greeks back to the mainland. When the suggestion was rejected, he himself withdrew together with the other contingents from the Peloponnese. On land, Pausanias, as regent for Pleistarchos, his cousin and Leonidas' son, led the army which won at Plataia. It was a brave but untidy victory, won as even Athenians conceded by 'the Dorian spear', but with no great display of Dorian brains; the story is confused but Pausanias must presumably take some of the blame for the fact that few of the Greeks seem to have known where they were or where they were going when the battle began.

But whether he knew where he was or not, whatever his generals' mistakes, the ordinary Spartan soldier was superb, at Plataia as he had been at Thermopylai. There are colourful stories in plenty about his courage ('So much the better if the Persians' arrows fill the sky, we shall fight in the shade'), but whether they are true or false the facts remain that at Thermopylai 300 were ordered to die and did as they were told, and that at Plataia 5,000 of them, though caught out of position, faced up to not less than five times their own number and routed them. 'The Persians', Herodotos says, 'were not inferior in boldness or strength . . . but they fell far short in skill.'

And so, in two seasons' fighting under Sparta, the Greeks had destroyed a Persian army and a Persian fleet, had cleared mainland Greece and the Aegean of the invaders and were well on the way to clearing Thrace, the Hellespont and the coast of Asia Minor. Fair-minded men shared the credit between the Athenian navy and the Spartan army, but, even with the credit shared, such an extraordinary achievement might, one would think, have earned for Sparta security, respect and a firm place at the head of her old League. In fact, within ten years the League had virtually disintegrated.

Why was this? Sparta's refusal to follow up the success in Asia Minor, contrasted with Athens' energetic creation of a new anti-Persian League, has been seen as the explanation, inaction interpreted as weakness leading to contempt and then hostility. There is truth in this, but it is not a simple story of the victory of a 'little Sparta party' over an 'expansionist party'. Sparta's debates were more complicated than that and it was not her decision so much as her wavering that caused the trouble.

For, firstly, three choices, not two, were open to her; to maintain her nominal hegemony at sea and if possible make it real; to leave the sea to Athens and extend her authority on land, taking advantage of the temporary confusion and weakness of the medising states of central and northern Greece, chief among them Boiotia and Thessaly; or to concentrate on repairing her still unsettled position inside the Peloponnese. And, secondly, she did not finally turn, perforce, to the third until she had alienated almost everyone and lost some three or four years in ineffectual dithering between the first and second.

The young ambitious regent, Pausanias, stood for the first. In 478 he took command of the allied fleet for a brilliantly successful season—Kypros and Byzantion were captured, but he was then recalled and Athens' leadership was established. Yet he was soon out in the east again 'as a private citizen', but surely not without some official support or without some purpose. Some time later he was recalled once more. Kleomenes' old protégé, Leotychidas, was no less clearly the champion of Kleomenes' old policy of landward expansion. The medisers were to be expelled and Ionians settled in their place; when the Ionians refused he lost interest in saving the east but not in securing the mainland—at some time between 478 and 476 he led an unsuccessful expedition into Thessaly. But just as Pausanias was recalled, so Leotychidas was exiled, in 476, and, Kleomenean to the last, took flight to Arkadia. Other Spartan actions of the period match: a stupid attempt to keep Athens weak by preventing the rebuilding of her walls after the Persian retreat could have been favoured by both parties; a proposal to exclude medisers from the Amphiktionic Council matches Leotychidas' schemes; a move to make war on Athens 'to recover the hegemony at sea', perhaps at about the same time as Leotychidas' exile, marks an obvious shift towards Pausanias. But the move came to nothing, the proposal was defeated, the attempt thwarted—by about 475 Sparta had gained nothing except the hostility of every state or group of states with which she had tried to interfere. More seriously, her consistent failure to achieve anything only exacerbated the old tensions which Kleomenes had created in the heart of the League itself.

In attempts to dominate at a distance, the allies might well see a clue to her future attitude nearer home, but they might also see a lesson in the fact that the attempts were failing. Nor is it likely that the domestic quarrelling went unnoticed by men who felt inclined to take advantage of it, men who now had two new encouragements to cause trouble. Some Athenians, not yet a majority, were sufficiently afraid of Spartan rivalry to take positive anti-Spartan action, chief among them Themistokles, the man who had built the Athenian fleet and won the battle of Salamis; and all Athenians had been experimenting for thirty years with a democratic form of government which seemed to be successful and was thoroughly alien to Spartan ways.

It is impossible to gauge the influence of Themistokles in stirring up hostility to Sparta inside the Peloponnese or to measure the amount of democratic feeling behind this hostility. But by about 470 Elis, the bulk of the Arkadian cities and an Argos which had almost recovered from Sepeia were in alliance against Sparta; Themistokles, whom ironically the Athenians themselves had ostracised, was helping to lead the alliance; and Argos, Elis and at least one of the major Arkadian cities had something which could be described as democratic constitutions.

For Sparta there was only one answer. Her problem was now purely

Peloponnesian and there could be no 'Great Sparta'. 'Little Sparta' more
or less had to start again from where she had been a century or more
ago. Her assets were a realisation that this was true, her army, and still
a certain amount of goodwill for her achievements in 480 and 479,
goodwill which was intense in some quarters, among those men in
every state who like her feared and disliked the new 'democratic' idea.
She may have had a further asset in a new Eurypontid king. Archidamos was presumably in theory reigning from the time of his grandfather Leotychidas' exile in 476 but in practice may not have become
influential before Leotychidas' death in 469. There is nothing in the
evidence to connect Archidamos with a change in Sparta's policy, but
there is no doubt that it is from about 470 that the story takes on a
different colour.

Pausanias was still alive and not without support, but soon after 470
the Spartans were persuaded rightly or wrongly that he was guilty
both of 'medism' (now presumably the desire to bring back the Persians
with Pausanias as their satrap) and of inciting the helots to revolt.
Pausanias died, unpleasantly. With or without Spartan encouragement
a new, aristocratically inclined government took over in Argos and
with Argos' defection some Arkadians began to waver—the Mantineans left the alliance. With definite Spartan collaboration, Athenian
aristocrats were enabled to condemn Themistokles, again for medism,
so that he had to run from the Peloponnese. The Arkadians were twice
defeated in battle, once at Tegea while Argos was still with them, once
alone, at Dipaia, in circumstances, now lost, which added that name to
the list of the Spartan hoplites' noted battle honours. By about 465 the
situation was saved; there is no way of knowing how far Spartan
authority was restored throughout the Peloponnese by these successes,
but the direct challenge to what was left of that authority had been met
and defeated. It was just in time.

Or perhaps not quite in time, for the great helot revolt which broke
out in 465 cannot be wholly unconnected with the troubles of the preceding years. The immediate reason for the uprising was an earthquake,
disastrous even if we are not inclined to believe the tales of 20,000 dead
and only five houses left standing. This was a tempting chance even
for an unincited helot. But although the charges of intriguing with the
helots which were brought against Pausanias are probably false, the
Arkadians at least must have tried to win some help from allies so near

at hand. There must have been trouble already in the air, even if it took an earthquake to make it real.

It was real enough when it came. The helots of Laconia were joined by those of Messenia and, what was more significant, by some of the *perioikoi* of the lower Pamisos valley. Sparta itself was saved by the quick-thinking of King Archidamos, and the helots, even with perioikic help, could not face the Spartan army in the field—though they did kill 300 Spartans in one engagement in the Stenyklaros plain. They retired, many presumably to the hills but the hard core to the natural fortress of Mount Ithome from which they could ignore Spartan hoplite skill and, in the absence of a full-scale blockade which was beyond Sparta's powers, threaten the greater part of the Pamisos valley.

Had Arkadia, Argos and Elis still been firm in their hostility, it is unlikely that Sparta would have survived; as things were, the earlier crisis had not been completely settled and the last battle with the Arkadians, at Dipaia, may be as late as 465, but the sting had been taken out of it. Argos stayed neutral, Mantinea actually sent help to the Spartans, so too did other allies, so too, though not without hesitation, did Athens, and against this opposition the helots could do nothing. By about 460, though still undefeated, the garrison in Ithome was forced to capitulate and leave the Peloponnese.

The Athenian intervention and its aftermath well illustrates the niceness of the balances involved. At Athens naval hegemony was now taken for granted, but some saw Sparta as an aggressively inclined threat to that hegemony; others did not and with a strong appeal to the sentiment that still survived from Plataia they managed to carry a majority with them. But at Sparta the enemies of Athens were strong enough, it was said, to win a decision to invade Attika when Athens herself was having trouble with one of her allies, Thasos; this even in the domestically black days of 465 (just before the earthquake). Whether the story is true or false the same men were able to work up enough resentment against the Athenian contingent which came to Ithome to send it home again, with its philo-Laconian leader, Kimon, on the absurd grounds that there was no further need of it (in fact for fear that it might take the Messenian side). At Athens again, this insult was enough to show that anti-Persian sentiment was out of date, and alliances were at once made with Sparta's enemies, with Thessaly and with Argos, where, significantly, it needed only this element of Athenian encouragement to revive traditional anti-Spartan feeling. And when the helots in Ithome, whom Athens had just been fighting, capitulated, it was Athens who took them in and found them a new home at Naupaktos on the north shore of the Korinthian Gulf.

The sketchiness of this account of the years after the triumph of 480 and 479 is inevitable. There is hardly a fixed point in the chronology of the period and it would need real precision to chart the ups and downs of Spartan feeling in what must have been a time of quick and subtle change. For the issues themselves cannot have been as clearcut to Spartans as they may seem to us—any Spartan would have hated an aggressive Athenian, but what of a tolerant Athenian, or a friendly Athenian? Did Leotychidas have many Athenian friends, Pausanias any?

Nor are the characters themselves much more than shadows. Of Leotychidas nothing is recorded; of Archidamos nothing substantial before 432; of Pausanias little beyond the official story which justified his extermination. According to that he was an arrogant traitor, arrogant already in 479 when he made a personal dedication at Delphi for the national victory at Plataia, a traitor not long after when from Byzantion he made contact with the Persian king and (more arrogance) proposed a marriage alliance with him. But how much truth was there in the official story? Thucydides recounts it as fact, Herodotos glances at it with more than a hint of doubt.

The few clues to the argument that survive are not illuminating. Sparta would be richer, said those who argued for war on Athens; but were they thinking of plunder or of tribute or of what? It may be the case that the economic development of Athens, League profits apart, was already taking her ahead of Sparta, but was it far enough ahead to be noticed, and were the Spartans or any other Greeks sophisticated enough to formulate the reasons? Probably not. By now the decline of local Spartan art in all departments was complete but, even if they notice such things, men do not want to make war about them. By now too the Lykourgan rules must have begun to set Spartans well apart from other prosperous Greeks in their daily life, but, given that Messenia and Laconia were still rich enough, as they surely were, to provide luxury if it was wanted, the reaction should have led to domestic reform, not to international ambition.

It may be that in another way the Lykourgan system was beginning to show a weakness which was having serious consequences by the fourth century. The number of full Spartan citizens, of the 'Equals', fell to something between a quarter or a half of what it had been in 479 and along with this went a considerable relative increase in the number of Spartans who were excluded from the privileged circle (below, p. 132 ff.). The tendency was probably already there a century earlier and the catastrophe of 465 would certainly focus attention on it, as it might dramatically accelerate any shift in numbers or proportions that there was. But again this is a domestic matter; sea hegemony or domination on the mainland was not obviously linked to problems either of population or of privilege.

On the other hand it is conceivable that the rules had had another more sinister effect, that they had already set Spartans so far apart from ordinary men that it is wrong to look for normal motives at all.

All nations have their myths. Britain stood alone in 1940—according to Churchill. Someone with a thought for the Commonwealth added 'alone, the whole 500,000,000 of us'. But the myth has won, not perniciously. Was the Spartan myth more pernicious?—that Leonidas and his 300 had marched out deliberately to certain death, that Spartans always came back from battle with their shields or on them. Natural and justified pride? or the first hint of that megalomaniac devotion to the idea of superiority without a purpose which is so marked in the Sparta of the later fifth and fourth centuries? The cult of military prowess leads, as Aristotle saw, to victory without any understanding of how to use it. The Spartans had certainly failed to profit from the victories of 480 and 479, but was the apparently random and ill-directed aggressiveness of the next twenty years an accidental or a natural consequence? Or is it that we do not know enough of the background?

Two things are reasonably firm. By 460 the old Peloponnesian alliance was more or less restored and there now existed a body of opinion which held that the maintaining of this alliance was a sufficient ambition. Secondly that the aggressive element was more and more coming to see Athens as the enemy no matter what direction the aggression might take. Both these views were imposed by events; the expansionism of the previous years had failed; whether it was to be renewed by land or by sea Athens would be involved, and, more immediately, thanks to the last folly of dismissing Kimon, Athens was now allied to Argos and already at war with some of Sparta's allies.

BIBLIOGRAPHY

For the Persian Wars and Sparta's part in them see A. R. Burn, *Persia and the Greeks* (1962) and, with more detail, C. Hignett, *Xerxes' Invasion* (1963); on relations with Arkadia, Argos and Athens, A. Andrewes, *The Phoenix 6* (1952) 1 ff., W. G. Forrest, *CQ* x (1961) 221 ff.; on chronology, A. W. Gomme, *Hist. Comm. on Thucydides* I (1945) 389 ff.; M. E. White, *JHS 84* (1964) 140 ff.; on the debate about hegemony, Forrest, *The Phoenix 21* (1967) 11 ff.

THE FIRST PELOPONNESIAN WAR AND AFTER

The so-called first Peloponnesian War which broke out in 459 with Athens' occupation of Megara and encounters with other northern allies of Sparta was an untidy affair from the Spartan side; more a series of adventures than a systematic war, and although the adventures were all at the time successful they did not add up to victory. The first, in 458, took a Spartan army into central Greece to support the supposed Dorian homeland, the little state of Doris, against Athenian-inclined Phokis, but led, as perhaps it was intended, to more important things, to the acquisition of a powerful ally, Boiotia, regularly hostile to Athens, more than ever suspicious of Athens as a democracy, and deeply concerned by the recent Atheno-Thessalian alliance. An attempt to help Boiotia's leading city, Thebes, consolidate her control over Tanagra towards the Athenian frontier, encouraged by the false hope of treachery in Athens itself, brought on a full-scale battle at Tanagra, and, hoplite against hoplite, the Spartans won. The adventure over, they went home—and two months later Athenian hoplites broke the Theban army at Oinophyta and took over the whole of Boiotia. Next, in about 448, an expedition across the Korinthian Gulf freed the Delphic oracle from the control of the Phokians and handed it over to the Delphians—shortly afterwards the Athenians returned it to the Phokians. The third adventure, in 446, was directed against an Athens which had lost Boiotia again in 447 and was now faced with a revolt among her allies of Euboia and in Megara. To take advantage of her troubles Pleistoanax, Pausanias' son and now the Agiad king, led a

Peloponnesian army into Attika and, without having taken any obvious advantage, led it back again.

Exhaustion after the helot revolt and fears about security inside the Peloponnese may explain this almost casual activity; at any rate the 'little Spartans' were on top. Substantially so, for spurs to action were not lacking; personal loss—Sparta's port, Gytheion, was ravaged by an Athenian naval force in 456; personal gain—the Persian king tried to provoke an invasion of Attika by bribery in 456; far more important, there were threats to the security of the League as a whole and to Sparta's prestige as its protector—Megara with its two ports, Nisaia and Pegai, Achaia, Troizen and, most damaging of all, the island of Aigina fell into Athenian hands, so closing the Isthmus and exposing all Sparta's northern allies to direct Athenian pressure.

And the Thirty Years' Peace which was signed after Pleistoanax' retreat from Attika was a 'little Spartans' ' peace. Athens had lost Megara and gave up its ports together with Troizen and Achaia, but she kept Aigina and, a powerful propaganda point, won for the first time a public admission that she had a right to rule her alliance even though the war against Persia for which the alliance had been created was ended (by the Peace of Kallias in 449). The leader of Greece against the Mede had become a power which could just, but only just, save its strictly Peloponnesian allies, but, in abandoning Aigina, could not quite save its face. There must have been many who in 446 had prayed with Pindar 'Keep this city [Aigina] in her voyage of freedom', and felt in 445 that more could have been done to answer the prayer.

There were certainly many in Sparta. We do not know why Pleistoanax left Attika in 446; the Athenian army may have come back from Euboia sooner than was expected, but it was allowed to return there without a fight and peace was concluded with a quickness and an air of easy compromise that gives some weight to the accusations of bribery that were brought against the king and his chief adviser, Kleandridas. Both were condemned and fled abroad. This need not mean that either was guilty but does mean that influential Spartans, specifically the ephors before whom the case would be heard, saw some unnecessary timidity in their behaviour, probably that the dominant pessimism of 459–446 had produced a natural reaction when the consequences were seen.

And this reaction seems to have been strong enough to push Spartan

debate on towards the issue which it faced in the months before the
real Peloponnesian War of 431. The 'whom to fight, if anyone?' of
479 had already become 'whether to fight Athens?'; now it was 'when
to fight Athens?'. It is likely that this was already the question in 440
when during the revolt of Samos from Athens the Peloponnesian
League was only prevented from helping Samos by the opposition of
the Korinthians; so at least the Korinthians claimed, clearly implying
that Sparta had favoured war. It certainly was the question in 432 when
the leading opponent of war, King Archidamos, could only argue:
'Let us send an embassy to state our charges firmly, while we look to
our resources; then, if Athens gives way, all is well; if not, in a year or
two we shall march against them with better hope'—Athens must give
way or be attacked. Perhaps delay was the most he could hope for
from a belligerent assembly, or perhaps even he believed that Sparta
had a genuine grievance. Did she?

Legally none. A neutral state, Korinth's colony Kerkyra, had appealed to Athens for help in a quarrel with her mother city; nothing in
the terms of the peace of 445 prevented such help and it was sent with
the strictest safeguards against provoking Spartan or any other reaction.
Other Athenian decisions followed, all against Korinthian interests,
some provocative but none contrary to the terms of the peace. The
Spartans themselves were later ready to admit that they had broken
the treaty when they invaded Attika in 431.

But in higher justice? Athens had been expanding, not at the direct
expense of Sparta but sometimes at the expense of Sparta's allies, and
persistent allied pressure, particularly Korinthian pressure, contributed
largely to her final decision. The choice appeared to lie between a
technically unjustified war and a serious risk of seeing the alliance dis-
integrate, a nasty dilemma. But although a first-class power may be
forgiven if it resents the slip to second-class status, the resentment can
hardly justify war so long as her rival observes the rules, as by and
large Athens had, ever since Sparta's own indecision in 478 had
allowed the creation of the Athenian League. In short the terrible
decision was taken out of pique and jealousy.

Not that the Spartans admitted either. As Thucydides says, 'the real,
but not the published, reason was Spartan fear of Athenian expansion'.
In public much was made of allied grievances and other things and
many may have deceived themselves into thinking that they had some

sort of right on their side. But the truth cannot have been buried very deep, no deeper perhaps than it is in the speech with which Archidamos' opponent, the ephor Sthenelaidas, won a vote for war:

I don't understand this talk. [Athenian envoys had just been arguing for arbitration.] They sing their own praises well enough, but they don't deny that they are wronging our allies and the Peloponnese. . . . Others may be rich in money, ships or cavalry but we are rich in fine allies and we must not abandon them. This is not a time for argument or arbitration . . . but for revenge, taken quickly and with all our strength. Let us not have any talk about thinking twice —it is the wrongdoers not the wronged who should think twice. You must vote now and vote like true Spartans, vote for war. Don't let Athens grow greater still. Don't abandon our allies. With God on our side let us attack.

Sthenelaidas won by a large majority. To Sparta hegemony mattered more than a treaty.

BIBLIOGRAPHY

On the events of 460–431, see *Hist. Comm. on Thucydides* by A. W. Gomme, I (1945); on the outbreak of war, A. Andrewes, *CQ* 9 (1959) 223 ff.

11

THE PELOPONNESIAN WAR I

The Spartan vote for war was confirmed at a meeting of the League assembly in the summer of 432, but time was needed to prepare an invasion and it was filled with a series of embassies to Athens making demands, some familiar and even reasonable, some new and preposterous. But they were all demands and Athens could see no reason to make concessions when, she thought, she had done no wrong—her answer, as before, was that she would accept arbitration.

The last demand, a new one, was that Athens should give up her empire—'there would be no war if Athens let the Greeks go free', a big step from war in defence of allies and the first sign of a new pose as liberator of Greece from Athenian tyranny, a pose, it was hoped, which would bring both neutrals and Athens' subjects over to Sparta's side. This was one of the two chief roads that might lead to victory. The other was that repeated invasion and devastation of Attika would either wear the Athenians down, a slim chance, or provoke them to a full-scale hoplite battle and almost certain defeat.

These were the only roads open. Her allies, chiefly Korinth, could muster a fleet of sorts but it could not compare in numbers or skill with that of Athens, nor was there any real hope that it could be increased by new building (Sparta had no source of revenue nor any reserve to compare with Athens' tribute and Athens' savings), or by finding new allies at a distance (the western Greeks, though some of them were well disposed enough, were not sufficiently concerned; the Persian king was not to be tempted to face the Athenians again and the embassies which went to Susa in the early years of the war came back empty-handed).

A simple plan, then: to attack by land and encourage disaffection. It ended in failure on both counts, though the arguments at the time could have seemed attractive. Behind their walls the Athenians were safe and, so long as the sea was theirs, would not go hungry; in fact they did stay behind their walls, but it was touch-and-go during the first invasion of 431 whether they would have the restraint to do so. Again, Athenian allies had not shown much public discontent at Athenian rule, nor did they during the war, but every allied city had its oligarchs, most of them unhappy and pro-Spartan, and these would be the men whom Spartans knew. They would not be likely to underrate the strength of their following when inviting Spartan intervention.

As in the Persian Wars a reasonable enough strategy (with the apparent odds on success rather higher), and as in the Persian Wars it was reasonably if cautiously applied. In the first few years the invasions struck hard at Athenian property and morale (in 429 there was no invasion but the Great Plague, a product of invasion conditions, was doing more harm to Athens than Spartans ever could), and although it could be argued that with a little more courage the Spartans might have set up a fort in Attika to keep up the pressure all the year round, as they did in 413, it is also true that the risks involved might have been too great. Elsewhere a serious attempt was made to put an end to increasing Athenian influence in north-west Greece, a sensitive spot for Korinth, and, surprisingly, in 427 a naval squadron was sent into the Aegean to support the revolt of one of Athens' major allies, Mytilene. Both efforts failed, but in 424 a small force marched to western Thrace, the only important area of Athens' empire which could be reached by land, and, although it did not receive the expected liberators' welcome, force, threats of force and an element of treachery brought many cities over, including the vital centre of Amphipolis. The adventure had been launched with hesitation—the force was made up of 700 helots armed with hoplite weapons and a hope of freedom together with 1,000 Peloponnesian mercenaries (no Spartan troops were to be risked)—and even when successful was hesitantly supported. But the risk was taken and it worked.

Indeed it decided the war after it had almost been decided the other way. From 431 to 425 invasion and the plague had been countered by Athenian raids on the coast of the Peloponnese which did no great damage. Nor did Argos, whom Athens probably hoped to lure into the war, show any signs of responding. But in 425 an Athenian force settled at Pylos on the west coast of Messenia and in a moment of folly Spartan troops were committed to the neighbouring island of Sphakteria where 120 of them were captured by the Athenians. The disgrace of surrender (against a background of the myth), an increasing shortage of manpower, whatever it was, Athens seemed to have won the war. But a ludicrously misconceived campaign in Boiotia led to a severe Athenian defeat at Delion in 424 and at the same time the Spartans appeared in Thrace. A compromise peace became possible and in 421 the first part of the war, the so-called Archidamian War, was brought to an end.

The expedition to Thrace was commanded by Brasidas, son of Tellis, the most outstanding and un-Spartan Spartan of the war—good general, able diplomat and honest man. He was lucky—he regularly 'happens to be' where he is most needed; brave, with a brilliant tactical and strategic eye and the boldness to act on what he saw; overconfident, perhaps, in his hopes of a ready welcome in Thrace but quick to adapt himself to what he found; above all, as Thucydides says, 'the first Spartan to go abroad and bring with him an impression of such general trustworthiness and reliability that men confidently expected the same virtues in those who followed him'. Other commanders had less talent and less virtue; Alkidas, for example, who led the naval expedition towards Mytilene, dithered hopelessly on the way and before returning slaughtered most of the prisoners he had taken, men whom he had come officially to liberate. Others again it is hard to judge; King Archidamos conducted the invasions of Attika before his death in 427 without alacrity but without obvious incompetence. Little more can be said.

Nor can we see behind the conduct in the field to the decision-making at home which directed it. During the Pylos crisis the 'authorities' intervened to take over from the commanders on the spot. When Athens' still loyal ally, Plataia, surrendered in 427, five 'judges' were sent from home and condemned Plataia and its population to destruction. No doubt these 'authorities' or 'judges' were or acted for that undefined group, 'the leading men', whose jealousy, Thucydides says, almost thwarted Brasidas' plans for Thrace, but what was a 'leading man'?

A king, of course, but not automatically. The office had its *auctoritas* and, given personal *auctoritas* as well, a king could readily become the 'leading man', but personal *auctoritas* was needed. The fact that so many royal figures of the fifth century were deposed, and the way in which they seem to be more and more submerged in party politics, do give some weight to Aristotle's claim that they were no more than hereditary military leaders. They were more than that, but neither Archidamos, defeated in the great debate of 432, nor his young successor Agis, nor the even younger Agiad Pausanias, who acted for his exiled father Pleistoanax until 426, nor the exile himself after his return are likely to have had any monopoly of power. Not that we simply put 'the ephors' in their place; a Sthenelaidas could make his mark and Brasidas as ephor in 429 is likely to have had a hand in rejecting Athenian peace overtures in that year (he was not a peaceful man). But a year of office could not make a comparative nonentity a 'leading man' for life. No, when Pindar singled out for praise at Sparta the 'counsels of the Elders' he put his finger on what must still have been the mainspring of policy-making, the *Gerousia*, and, behind the *Gerousia*, the tight and ever tightening circle of noble families which could hope to provide its members. Here an Archidamos or a Brasidas would have his powerful friends and enemies, but of their identity there is no trace.

Nor of their opinions. Some may have been reluctant to fight in 431 and others may have come to regret the decision quite soon. Many more, a majority, were shocked by the calamity of Pylos into a willingness for peace, and offers were made, unrealistic but not necessarily ungenuine. It will have been the same men who secured the recall of King Pleistoanax from exile—he had arranged peace before and might do so again—and, with Brasidas' successes to sober the Athenians and his death to weaken the war-party at home, they were in the end successful.

Their case was overwhelming. In 421 Sparta's position in the Peloponnese was as critical as it had been in the 460's. Pylos, which the Athenians had cleverly garrisoned with Messenians from Naupaktos, was fomenting Messenian disaffection, and the extent of Sparta's fear on that score is shown not only by her readiness to despatch 700 of the more energetic helots with Brasidas but by a sickening massacre of some 2,000 more—'they offered freedom', says Thucydides, 'to those who claimed to have served them best in war, thinking that those who came forward would be the likeliest to revolt. Some 2,000 were selected, paraded around the temples in garlands as if set free, and then wiped out. No one ever knew how each was killed.' Further afield, not all of her allies shared the Korinthian enthusiasm for war and some had sizable democratic elements which were more likely than not to favour Athens (Megara almost deserted in 424). Elis was more concerned to expand southwards into Triphylia than to fight for Sparta; Arkadian Tegea and Mantinea to fight each other—they did in 423 and Mantinea went on to annex Parrhasia, an area to the west of Mainalon. Problems like these could not be dealt with while attention was focussed on a war with Athens. Meanwhile the thirty-year truce which had been negotiated with Argos in 450 was nearing its end. Argos had not responded to Athenian suggestions that she ignore the truce, but she was not likely to forego the chance that 420 would bring of fishing in troubled Arkadian waters.

On the other hand it could have been argued that the peacemakers were wrong. The best that could be hoped for, and all that was promised in the peace, was a simple exchange, Pylos for Amphipolis. Korinth had lost much and regained nothing, Boiotia could not be persuaded that there was not more to be won after her victory at Delion; others were similarly let down. For them, less directly for all, anything short of outright victory was an admission of failure, an admission that Sparta did not deserve her hegemony, and so long as there was the faintest hope of victory, as Brasidas and his friends will have argued there still was, she should have fought on.

In a sense this was true, but the real error lay back in 432 with those who had committed Sparta to fight in the first place. However reasonable the plans may have seemed, they were based on misjudgments, of the temper of Athens and of Athens' allies. The odds on victory were just not high enough, when not only victory but a handsome victory was essential. Better by far to enjoy the fruits of Laconia and Messenia and let Korinth and others go their own way, than to face both a guilty conscience and the loss of very much more.

BIBLIOGRAPHY

For the events of the war, Thucydides with Gomme's Commentary, II and III; for Spartan strategy, P. A. Brunt, *The Phoenix 19* (1965) 255 ff.

12

THE PELOPONNESIAN WAR II

As Thucydides saw, the war which began again in 415 and ended with the fall of Athens in 404 was one with the war of 431–421; ten years of fighting had hardened the opposition between the two great powers, had sharpened the distinctions between them for other Greeks to note, oligarch and democrat, had defined the slogans behind which they would fight—'liberation of the Greeks' was formally abandoned by Sparta in 421 but it lay ready to hand for reassertion. It would be wrong though to think that either looked on the peace at the time as a temporary affair. Athens had confirmed her right to Empire and could turn her thoughts again to building programmes and the like; Sparta had plenty to occupy her in the Peloponnese and with a characteristic mixture of hesitation, cunning and brutality set to work to salvage what she could from the wreck of her alliance.

For lesser allies, brutality; the Mantineans were ejected from Parrhasia; Elis had been thwarted over Triphylia. For the greater, diplomacy and courage. There was much indecision over how the game should be played (for the year immediately after the peace the assembly elected at least two ephors who were opposed to it), but the situation almost demanded indecision. To keep Athens well disposed (peace was followed within a few months by formal alliance), Argos neutral (there were some Argives who favoured Sparta), and at the same time to make Korinth and Boiotia realise that their real interests still lay with Sparta (the Athenian alliance reminded them of the old tag that together Sparta and Athens could rule the whole of Greece), this was the problem and, if the delicate manœuvrings of 421–418 failed to produce the perfect result, they came as near to it as was humanly possible. In 418 an army of Spartans, Boiotians and Korinthians marched out against an unsteady Argos which had only minimal Athenian support.

The battle of Mantinea was the first large-scale Spartan engagement since Tanagra in 457. By the time it was fought the Boiotian and Korinthian contingents had returned home and, with some Arkadians, Sparta was alone. The Spartan command, in this case Agis, Archidamos' son, was as so often hesitant, even incompetent, but the Spartan hoplite triumphed and in one day the disgrace of Pylos was wiped out, the almost forgotten glory of Plataia restored.

And it is a mark of some distinction, also no doubt of relief after the razor's-edge diplomacy of the preceding years, that the victory was followed not by any rash assertion of recovered authority but by a moderate peace with Argos, including, a new idea, the declaration of a kind of Monroe Doctrine for the Peloponnese; at the same time Athens' part in the battle was ignored. Since Sparta had conspicuously failed to keep or to enforce on her allies the keeping of several terms of the peace of 421, this silence about Athens was no more than politic, and the idea that Peloponnesian brothers should stand united against the outside world did not mark any great change of heart—in the year after Mantinea 'the Spartans settled affairs in Achaia which had not been previously to their taste' (Thucydides).

This with other Spartan intervention, to help oligarchs in Sikyon and in Argos itself, shows what Sparta really meant by Peloponnesian solidarity. But it was something that she limited herself to the Peloponnese and, on the surface, there was a better chance of stable peace in Greece after 418 than there had been for nearly sixty years. Argos soon reverted to her traditional anti-Spartan line and many Athenians shared Argos' views, but it was only when Athens made herself weak as well as hostile that the temptation became too great and the second stage of the Peloponnesian War began.

In 415 Athens committed a large part of her forces to an attack on Sicily, specifically on Sicily's richest city, the Korinthian colony of Syracuse. At Sparta a natural sympathy of Dorian for Dorian and the fear of further Athenian expansion was reinforced by the temporary weakening of Athens and by the bellicose advice of an Athenian deserter, the energetic, clever and unscrupulous Alkibiades. Only conscience stood in the way, but that was stilled in 414 when an Athenian force joined with the Argives in a raid on the Laconian coast. This time Athens had put herself in the wrong and Alkibiades could be heeded.

As he had suggested a Spartan officer was sent at once to help the Syracusans, Gylippos, son of Kleandridas the exile of 446, and preparations began for an invasion of Attika. In the following spring King Agis led the Peloponnesian army north but not, as his father Archidamos had, for a mere destructive raid. They carried with them the makings of a weapon much more dangerous than hoplite spears—tools and materials to build a permanent fort at Dekeleia in northern Attika, not much more than ten miles from the walls of Athens. So the Athenians were forced to man their walls winter and summer alike, were robbed of all Attika and were cut off from one of their main supply-lines, the overland route to Euboia. Their slaves could desert and their oligarchs could think of revolution. This was to be a very different war.

In other important ways it was different too. In 413 the Athenian forces in Sicily were wiped out; at one stroke Athenian naval, financial and moral supremacy was gone. Among her allies neither fear nor greed was a motive for loyalty; only affection or habit. The alliance did hold astonishingly well but Sparta's slogan of freedom for the Greeks now had a real chance of falling on willing ears. Persia too was stirred by Athens' defeat. Hitherto, with minor slips on both sides, the peace of 449 had held and a series of Spartan embassies in the early years of the war had failed to move her. But now the Great King's representatives in Asia Minor were ready to bargain, their offer money, their price control of the Greek cities of Asia Minor.

For Sparta, then, the road to victory was straight and open. While Agis kept up pressure from Dekeleia she need only assemble a fleet, maintain it with Persian silver, and spread revolt from Athens through the Aegean. Only one first step was needed, that the 'liberators of Hellas' should be ready to hand over Greeks to barbarians, and it was a step that the first envoys of the 'liberators' readily took. Some Spartans on the spot and no doubt many more at home took little pleasure in 'fawning on the barbarian for silver', as one put it, and preferred the idea of peace with Athens, but an agreement was made with the Persians in 412 which began with the clause 'Such land and cities as the King holds and such as his fathers held shall belong to the King' and, reinterpretation, modification and misgiving though there was, the concession held.

Even so, victory was not so near as it seemed. Athens' allies did not desert *en bloc* or willingly; Persian deviousness and internal Persian squabbling and jealousy made the silver hard to come by; the Athenians, with extraordinary resilience and courage, built a new fleet and still kept some of their skill in using it; and there was Alkibiades.

While Agis lay at Dekeleia, so the story ran, Alkibiades at Sparta had lain with Agis' wife. But fear of retribution, together with a natural distaste for Sparta's sober habits, and perhaps, to be fair, a touch of remorse, turned his mind to Athens again. He was sent out with the first Spartan fleet to Asia in 412 and served it well enough, but contact and success with the Persian governor, Tissaphernes, soon turned Sparta's agent into a Persian adviser, and the advice, at first neutral ('play each side off against the other'), acquired a positively pro-Athenian tone when there seemed to be a chance of buying return to Athens in exchange for Persian help. The return was achieved even though the help was not forthcoming and so from 411 until his second exile in 407 Athens not Sparta had the benefit of Alkibiades' talents. Even with suspicious and half-hearted support from home, they were more than a match for any commander that Sparta could send out against him.

The admirals to whom Sparta entrusted the east Aegean year by year from 412 were, naturally, inexperienced; they were also brutal or incompetent or both. They won few friends and fewer battles. The most attractive of them was Kallikratidas (406) who did have the spirit to complain when kept waiting for his Persian money, but one cannot admire too much an admiral who falls off his ship and is drowned while losing an important battle (at Arginoussai). Of the others, Astyochos in 412 was prepared to hand over the captured Ionian city of Iasos to Tissaphernes and sell him the population; his successor Mindaros in 411 and 410 managed to lose the whole of his fleet at the battles of Kynossema and Kyzikos, so giving Athens a breathing space of two years before another Peloponnesian fleet could be assembled; while the general standard of Spartan command can be judged by the famous message sent back to Sparta by Mindaros' second-in-command after Kyzikos—'Ships lost; Mindaros dead; men starving; no idea what to do'.

One man stands out, Lysander. As a commander his record may not be striking, one minor and one major naval victory against incompetent opposition, one unnecessary defeat on land which lost him his life (in 395), but as a diplomat and organiser his performance was almost flawless, unless we count arrogance, dishonesty, unscrupulousness and brutality as flaws. During his first command, in 407, he quickly won the confidence and full support of the young Persian prince Kyros who had then taken over the Persian command in Asia Minor; sank fifteen Athenian ships at Notion, thus indirectly causing the second exile of Alkibiades from Athens; and began to build up the personal following among the extreme oligarchs of the Greek cities which, when they later came to power, turned the Aegean into something like a private empire. That the loyalty was to Lysander not to Sparta is shown clearly enough by their and Kyros' refusal to co-operate with Kallikratidas the new commander of 406, and by the agitation which led to Lysander's reappearance, technically as an adviser, in fact for an illegal second term as commander in 405. At once the fleet's enthusiasm and finances revived and by a clever trick it destroyed or captured all but a tiny remnant of the Athenian navy at Aigospotamoi; 3,000 Athenian prisoners were massacred; other Athenians abroad, soldiers, officials, settlers, were herded back to Athens; a Spartan commander (called a *harmostes*) and a group of ten oligarchs (a *dekarchy*), Lysander's friends, were installed in many of the cities; Lysander's fleet sailed into the Saronic Gulf; and Athens was starved into accepting the same conditions, a Spartan garrison and an oligarchic government.

Throughout this story of the last years of the war there are frequent references in the sources to official action or decision at Sparta, by the ephors or by the 'government', but there is no clue to the nature of any debate, except perhaps in the opposition between Lysander and Kallikratidas and the latter's willingness to talk of peace with Athens (reasonable terms were in fact offered after both Kyzikos and Arginoussai so Kallikratidas was not alone). King Pleistoanax's past and the future of his son, Pausanias, who succeeded in 408, might make one suspect that the Agiads were for peace, Agis' links with Alkibiades (before the scandal) and with Lysander, and the enthusiasm he showed at Dekeleia might mean that he favoured submission to Persia and war to the end, but this is guesswork.

However, no matter how they were arrived at, the conditions of peace finally imposed on Athens were far from harsh; she lost her walls, her navy and her democracy, and she acquired a garrison; that was all. Against the Korinthians and the Boiotians who demanded complete destruction the Spartans argued that Athens' services to Greece in the past should earn her mercy, and although it is easy to see a more cynical motive, the desire to make Athens a loyal servant of Spartan policy in Central Greece against possible Boiotian expansion, it is not unreasonable to think that some Spartans still had some decency.

BIBLIOGRAPHY

For the events, Thucydides bks V–VIII with commentary by A. W. Gomme, A. Andrewes and K. J. Dover (forthcoming); Xenophon, *Hellenica*, bks I and II. A recent detailed study of Lysander, D. Lotze, *Lysander und der Pelop. Krieg* (1964).

13

SPARTA'S EMPIRE

In the year that followed the peace Athenian exiles, with Boiotian help, returned to Attika and challenged the thirty oligarchs whom the Spartans had set up in Athens. Lysander and King Pausanias led rival expeditions to help the oligarchs, but Pausanias used the chance to negotiate a settlement. The Thirty fled, democracy was restored, a general amnesty proclaimed. This little episode well illustrates the complexity of the problems that Sparta's too complete victory raised.

Some things that had always been clear were still clear, for example that the Peloponnese must be secure—probably in 400 (the exact date is uncertain) King Agis led an army north to punish Elis for earlier disloyalty, to 'bring her to her senses' as Xenophon puts it. But further afield things were not so easy. The slogan of 'liberation' had been forgotten for the Asiatic Greeks in 412; in 404 it was ignored for all. Lysander's puppet oligarchs were tied to Sparta far more firmly than any of her so-called subjects had been tied to Athens; they were hated in their cities both as puppets and as oligarchs and through them Sparta was hated too.

Then excessive power bred fear, fear of Sparta among her stronger and more independent allies, fear of Lysander in Sparta itself. Korinthians and Boiotians who would have welcomed the destruction of Athens in 404 saw in oligarchic Athens just the Spartan satellite they had feared—hence the Boiotian help to the returning exiles, Korinthian and Boiotian refusal to join in 'bringing Elis to her senses', and a few years later a Korinthian-Boiotian-Athenian alliance. Some Spartans,

among them Pausanias and possibly even Agis as well, disapproved of
Lysander's methods and suspected his motives—hence Pausanias' arbitration in Athens, where a majority of the ephors shared his views, and,
about the same time, some moves against the dekarchies elsewhere.

So, much as in 479, when single-minded brutality might have
worked, indecisive aggressiveness merely won enemies for Sparta and
at the same time gave those enemies heart. They were heartened still
more when the aggressiveness came to the fore again in 401 and Sparta
decided to meddle in Persian politics as well.

The collaboration with Persia had depended on two men, Lysander
and Kyros. Lysander stopped short, as yet, of any claim to rule at home
though when Agis died in 399 he did succeed in putting his friend,
Agis' brother Agesilaos, on the throne by challenging the legitimacy of
the heir apparent (Alkibiades' intrigue with Agis' wife still had its
uses). But Kyros wanted the Persian throne for himself and thought
that he could claim Spartan support in an attempt to dethrone his
elder brother. More surprisingly, Sparta gave the support he wanted
and, hesitantly as ever, supported him well enough to lead her to war
with Persia when he lost. Nor is it possible to blame Lysander and his
friends alone for the mistake; no Spartan who still believed in freedom
for Greeks, who still shared Kallikratidas' views, is likely to have stood
out very strongly against the sending of a Spartan fleet to intimidate
barbarians even if on another barbarian's behalf. Kyros, after all, had
kept his word, his troops were largely Greek and his victims were not.

But Kyros lost and his brother, Artaxerxes, re-established himself in
Asia Minor with no goodwill to Greeks or Spartans. So, in 400,
suddenly remembering that Greeks had a right to be free, Sparta began
another war of liberation in Asia Minor, this time with Persia as her
opponent and was eager enough about it to send Agesilaos (with
Lysander as adviser) to Asia (in 396). This was a distraction which
could only encourage her other enemies to open opposition. Three
years later she was at war at home with Boiotia, Korinth and Athens.

In her defence it could be said that most stories put down the outbreak of this, the Korinthian War, to provocative Boiotian intrigue in
central Greece, encouraged by Persian bribery; that the intervention in
Asia Minor was an easy consequence of the support to Kyros and at the
same time a sign that Sparta had repented of her earlier betrayal of the
Greeks; that the support to Kyros might have been given out of loyalty

and gratitude. In other words a certain amount of vacillation and a slightly foolhardy devotion to her friends might be the only charges that could be brought against her. But she was quite ready to sell the Asiatic Greeks to Persia again a year or two later—the repentance does not seem to have been all that genuine—and her innocence in the preliminaries of the Korinthian War can be doubted. Many blamed the Boiotians, but some blamed Sparta, specifically Lysander; it was an ally of Sparta, Phokis, which actually opened the fighting; and even the most pro-Spartan source, Xenophon, admits that the Spartans were glad to have an excuse to punish the Boiotians for their recent disloyalty. If so, there is a strong hint of madness. Spartans had long believed that they had a right to rule, but most of them had set some limits to their hegemony, some of them a reasonable limit, the Peloponnese. Now it seems as if the success of 404 had turned their heads completely.

Many ancient historians also saw 404 as a moment of change. Remembering an old saying that lust for wealth would be Sparta's ruin they argued that the wealth brought back by Lysander from abroad corrupted Lykourgan simplicity and led to the great defeat at Leuktra (in 371). The story is overdramatic and oversimplified. Also, under the influence of the myth, it gets the emphasis wrong. New wealth there was, not only from Lysander but from Agesilaos' campaign in Asia and from the tribute which Sparta now exacted from her new empire, but if it corrupted it did so because Lykourgos' régime had made Spartans corruptible. Nor was wealth the only corrupter. It was as much the inflexibility of the system as the personal weakness of those who lived under it that caused the trouble.

It is probably no accident that the first agitation that we hear of in Sparta by the underprivileged other than helots was in 398. Then a plot was discovered for helots, *perioikoi* and other oppressed groups to set upon their masters, its leader a certain Kinadon, a Spartan but not one of the 'Equals'. Kinadon and some associates were quickly put to death and nothing more is heard of revolution.

Kinadon was to have relied on two classes other than helots and *perioikoi*, *hypomeiones* ('inferiors') and *neodamodeis* ('new citizens'). The former, mentioned only in this context, are usually thought to have been those demoted from full citizenship for failure to maintain their Lykourgan obligations. To their number there is no clue. The latter are more familiar, helots enrolled for military service with a promise of freedom and some status in the community in return, and were probably more numerous, for 700 were sent with Brasidas to Thrace in 424, the first known example of the practice, 2,000 with Agesilaos to Asia, and there are other substantial groups. But the status they acquired for risking their lives was not that of 'Equal'; in 418 the survivors from Thrace are still fighting in a separate unit, not mixed with the 'Equals', and Kinadon links them with the other depressed, as men who would gladly eat a Spartiate raw.

There was, then, unrest at the lower levels of Spartan society. There may also have been some tension higher up, though it is hard to assess. The apparently increasing vulnerability of the kings to magisterial and other pressure; the appearance of powerful non-royal figures like Brasidas or Lysander; the much greater frequency with which the ephors are named as taking this or that action, this or that initiative, the closeness of the control they seem to have over commanders abroad; all this may be a false impression created by the much greater detail of our narratives for the period after 431 and even more after 411 when Xenophon takes up the story (after all Chilon was not a king, Kleomenes was tried and went into exile, the ephors bullied Anaxandridas), but it may mean something more, that power was slowly shifting away from the traditional families towards others, still Spartiate, but not of the inner circle. It is to be noted that Aristotle sees the ephors of his day as belonging to a much wider class than the *Gerousia*.

To come back to the point, there may have been some movement, there was certainly some unease in Spartan society and both will have become more noticeable after 404. So too did the misbehaviour of Spartans and of Sparta. But it was not greed for wealth or the effect of wealth alone that was responsible, it was a new range of demands of all sorts suddenly imposed on men and on a system too uncivilised to cope with them. Nor, for the most part, did these demands do more than accentuate faults that were already there. There had been nothing quite like the arrogance of many of Lysander's harmosts; like the conceit of King Agesilaos who in leaving for Asia thought of himself as a second Agamemnon setting out for Troy; like the megalomania of those who 'welcomed' war with the strongest powers in Greece at the same time as a war with Persia. But Kleomenes, the regent Pausanias and the ephor Sthenelaidas had all shown symptoms in their day. And the saying that greed would be Sparta's ruin which first appears in the seventh century was presumably as much an observation as an oracle.

Aristotle gave the proper summary: 'the Spartans always prevailed in war but were destroyed by empire simply because they did not know how to use the leisure they had won, because they had practised no more fundamental skill than skill in war'. And the next twenty-five years is little more than a sad catalogue of instances. Lysander was killed at Haliartos in 395 while engaged in a foolish foray against the Boiotians, his opponent Pausanias was exiled for failing to give him proper support. Pausanias employed his leisure in compiling an attack on Lykourgos' laws; the reputation of Lysander was blackened, in Spartan eyes, by the 'discovery' after his death that he had intrigued for an elective kingship with himself as the first candidate—true or false, a further sign that Lykourgan rigidity was under some strain. But on the surface all soon became smooth again for Agesilaos, the man whom Lysander manœuvred on to the throne to be his pliant collaborator, turned out to be one of the strongest and ablest of Sparta's kings.

A shrewd, devious but decisive politician, an excellent general, he held Sparta to a more or less consistent policy with surprisingly little indecision or self-contradiction till his death, as a very old man, in 360. The only trouble was that he settled on a mistaken policy. In essence it was to sell the Asiatic Greeks once more to Persia, buying in return complete Persian support for Spartan rule in Greece. This rule was to be based on the Persian enforced principle of autonomy for the Greek states, interpreted to mean that Sparta could control her dependencies as before but that no other state could acquire or maintain a hold even over willing allies, above all that Thebes, which Agesilaos saw, rightly if obsessively, as the chief threat to Spartan domination, should not be allowed to preserve the Boiotian League of which she was the leader.

The idea was accepted when it was seen that the war could not be won. A crushing defeat at sea at the hands of a Persian fleet under Athenian command (at Knidos, 394) started the disintegration of the overseas empire. An equally striking victory on land (at Nemea in 394) led to no more than a stalemate in mainland Greece. Thereafter it took some time to persuade Artaxerxes that the Spartans had changed once more but at last the persistence of an able Spartan diplomat, Antalkidas, and the rather too independent behaviour of a resurgent Athens, won him over. In 387 he 'sent down' his terms to the Aegean—

the Greeks of Asia were to be his, there should be peace and autonomy throughout Greece, and he himself would make war on any who refused the terms. Make war, Xenophon says, 'together with those who wished', but Ephoros had a slightly different formula, 'through the agency of those who wished', one which points a little more clearly to Sparta's intended role as arbiter of the new dispensation.

There is a story that Agesilaos was accused of medising. 'Not at all', he replied, 'it is the Medes who are laconising', and so indeed they were. With the threat of Persia hanging over them Thebes, Athens, Korinth and Argos had no choice but to fall in with Agesilaos' grotesque abuse of the principle of autonomy. During the Korinthian War, Korinth had become a democracy and entered into a political union with Argos; now the union was dissolved and Korinth became again an 'autonomous' oligarchy and a member of Sparta's League. Thebes lost Boiotia, and Athens, although not suffering directly, had to tread very warily in any attempts to restore her fifth-century alliances in the Aegean. This, however, was only a beginning. Probably in 385 autonomous democratic Mantinea was attacked, destroyed and replaced by five 'autonomous' oligarchic villages, as it had been before its synoecism of nearly a century before; autonomous democratic Phleious was ordered to take back oligarchic exiles, then later (in 381) besieged and left with a Spartan garrison to guarantee the 'autonomy' of its new oligarchy; another garrison was established (in 382) in the citadel of Thebes by methods which even the Spartans publicly disowned—a Spartan officer, Phoibidas, passing through Boiotia, took advantage of the treachery of Theban oligarchs—but although Phoibidas was fined, the garrison was not withdrawn and some suspected that Phoibidas, a friend of Agesilaos, had not acted entirely on his own initiative; further afield, a major expedition was sent north in 382 to break up a fast-growing confederation of the cities of Chalkidike and the neighbourhood under the leadership of Olynthos and in 379 the separate cities, 'autonomous' once more, were admitted to the Spartan alliance; in 378 another would-be Phoibidas, Sphodrias, tried his hand at an unscheduled attack on Peiraieus and, although it was a fiasco, intrigue at home won him lighter treatment than Phoibidas had received—he was acquitted. Behind these examples of brutality and aggressiveness there is a pattern.

On the one hand, behind the cynical disregard for the spirit of the king's principle of autonomy there seems to be a new attitude towards the allies. The synod of the League still met and took decisions but there is a difference of tone between the meeting of 432 where allied voices still mattered and that of 382 (before the attack on Olynthos) where, Xenophon says, 'most supported an expedition but mainly because they wanted to please the Spartans'. It is not surprising that the last recorded meeting of the League is not far in the future, and symptomatic that in 382 it was decided to replace the statutory provision of troops by member-states with a monetary equivalent with which mercenaries could be hired. A concession no doubt to the allied farmers and artisans who were irked by constant service and yet mocked by the Spartans for their amateurishness, but also a further concentration of power in the hands of the state which employed the mercenaries as its own. There is a difference in the level of intolerance which Sparta showed to the independent-minded—Mantinea had been punished before but not as she was in 385. And as great a difference in the treatment of new allies—the formula which the cities of Chalkidike swore 'to follow wherever the Spartans might lead' was not new but it now meant what it said. It was a clear commitment to subjection.

On the other hand the new security and strength inside the Peloponnese were being used in the main against Thebes. Olynthos had shown signs of pro-Theban feelings and even Sphodrias' attack on Attika came after Athens had repaid the debt of 403 by helping an anti-Spartan coup in Thebes.

Behind the pattern there was Agesilaos. He was in charge of the application of the Peace of 487; again at Phleious; Phoibidas was his friend, perhaps a relative; Sphodrias owed him his acquittal. There was indeed an opposition, led at first by Agesipolis, who took the place of his exiled father Pausanias in 395 and died before Olynthos in 380, and then by Pausanias' younger son Kleombrotos, but its influence on policy was neither firm nor lasting enough to let its character show clearly in the sources. It has been argued that Agesipolis approved of real autonomy for the Greeks (though he did not refuse the command at Mantinea or at Olynthos) and there are some hints that he was more sympathetic than Agesilaos to independent-minded democratic elements in the allied cities, as his father Pausanias was to the Athenian democrats in 403; Kleombrotos was certainly less obsessed by Thebes than was Agesilaos and perhaps more anxious to curb Athens. But it is risky to elevate what may be no more than differences of emphasis into a coherent policy, to argue that the Agiads advanced allied interests by diverting Sparta from land campaigns against Thebes to a naval war against Athens because that would make smaller demands on them.

At least it must be said that by supporting Sphodrias' acquittal Agesilaos showed himself as ready as anyone to provoke Athens, and Athens was provoked. For three years Sparta fought her and Thebes together with something less than success against either (significantly a force of 1,000 Spartan hoplites was defeated by 300 Thebans at Tegyra in 375) and in 375 the Peace of 387 was renewed with Sparta no longer its arbiter. On at least two points she had to give way; garrisons in foreign cities, such as hers in many cities of Boiotia and elsewhere, were an infringement of autonomy; and Athens was as free to maintain what had suddenly grown into an extensive alliance in the Aegean as was Sparta to hold the Peloponnese. Then, extraordinarily (megalomania again?), after little more than a year of peace, she replied to a minor, perhaps even unintentional, Athenian misdemeanour (the restoration of some democratic exiles to the island of Zakynthos) by mounting a large naval expedition against Athenian interests in the Adriatic in concert with Dionysios, the tyrant of Syracuse (in 373). The expedition accomplished nothing and withdrew with heavy losses. Sparta was at war again.

In this assault on Athens one might see the hand of Kleombrotos and his friends. In 376 Agesilaos had fallen ill and recovered only slowly. Thereafter the attacks on Thebes were less vigorous and in 375, wisely but uncharacteristically, the Spartans refused, after a long debate, an invitation to interfere with one of Thebes' strongest allies, Jason of Thessalian Pherai. At the same time pressure on Athens was increased and, apart from the interlude of peace, was kept up until the next peace conference, at Sparta, in summer 371, when Agesilaos himself first re-appears. But it is to be noted that while peace was being discussed at Sparta Kleombrotos himself was in Phokis with an army some 10,000 strong, a large force if its intentions were purely to defend the Phokians from Theban inroads. Nor did Agesilaos initiate the peace moves. That was Athens' doing, herself becoming suspicious of Theban expansion, and it was Athenian diplomacy that persuaded the Spartans (and the Thebans present) to accept yet another settlement.

Agesilaos' claim to distinction was rather different. By harking back to 387 and insisting on the independence of the Boiotian cities he drove

Thebes from the peace, and he must have been among the eager majority who voted in the Spartan assembly a few days later that Kleombrotos and his army should invade Boiotia to secure this independence. One Spartan, Prothous (his name deserves to be recorded), argued for delay followed by a general Greek campaign if Thebes persisted, but he, they thought, 'was talking nonsense'. Kleombrotos was ordered to advance and at Leuktra he and the Spartan element in his army was destroyed by Theban hoplites.

It is hard to say who was most surprised, Sparta, the rest of Greece or the Thebans themselves. In a daze the Spartans sent another army towards Boiotia but it came to its senses in time and turned back; incredulously the Athenians sent away the Boiotian herald who came to announce the victory and set about organising yet again a general peace; at a complete loss the Thebans bogged themselves down in Boiotian politics. But the hard fact came through, Sparta was beaten. And as it dawned, city after city (except Athens, increasingly conscious of Theban power) showed in its instinctive jubilation just what the Spartan rule of the last thirty, in many cases of the last 200 or 300, years had meant. The celebrations of 404 had been real enough, but mainly confined to the victors over Athens, the celebrations of 1945 were real enough but in the main they happened with a victorious foreign army in attendance. In 371–70 Sparta's own allies, with no Thebans in sight, went wild, and when a Theban army did appear in the Peloponnese in 370, alien though it was, it found an easy passage to the banks of the Eurotas. An Arkadian League founded itself without much help, Messenia was refounded as an independent state with Theban blessing (presumably with much Theban advice, for 300 years of slavery does not produce a ready or competent government). Sparta was back to where she had been around 750 B.C. Why?

BIBLIOGRAPHY

For the events see Xenophon, *Hellenica* II–VI, Diodoros xiv–xv and Plutarch *Lysander, Agesilaus, Pelopidas*. On Spartan domestic politics, R. E. Smith, *CP* 43 (1948) 145 ff. and *Historia* 2 (1953–4) 274 ff.; on the organisation of her empire, H. W. Parke *JHS 50* (1930) 37 ff.; on international negotiations, T. T. B. Ryder, *Koine Eirene* (1965).

EXCURSUS II

THE POPULATION

It is easy enough to explain the defeat itself—as early as 390 new tactics had caught the Spartans off guard at Lechaion, in 371 the Thebans used still newer tactics and the Spartan hoplite, splendid though he was, could not cope. One Theban section of the line, fifty deep, was too much for a traditional Spartan depth of about twelve. For all their skill in detail Spartan commanders had ignored the military advances of the previous fifty years. It is easy too to explain the delight of Sparta's so-called allies at the defeat—quite simply they had been asked to do too much, they had been consulted too little, and even when it was they who profited and their enemies who suffered, they had probably felt that the enemies suffered too much. Easy again to see why one defeat should seem so shattering—the myth did not allow defeat at all.

But it is not so easy to understand why it should not only seem but be so shattering, why Sparta was broken for good by Leuktra and the loss of Messenia, why she was internally too weak to survive the shock. This weakness, a shortage of manpower, has already been alluded to; the problems that it raises are best treated outside the narrative.

Here at the outset there are perplexing ambiguities in the words that our sources use to describe all or part of the population of Laconia. *Lakedaimonios* and the less frequent *Lakon* can be used of any inhabitant of Laconia, *perioikos* or Spartan, but the plural *Lakedaimonioi* is frequently used of the Spartans alone as well as of a mixed force. *Spartiates* on the other hand often means Spartan but usually has a narrower reference and describes only full Spartan citizens, i.e. the 'Equals'. The former

doubt usually makes it impossible to measure the Spartan as opposed
to perioikic element in any numbered 'Lakedaimonian' army, the latter
obscures both the existence and the strength of non-'equal' elements in
Sparta itself, or in the army. These elements, *hypomeiones* and *neo-*
damodeis, have already been described (p. 124 f.), and some would argue
that the decrease of Spartan proportions in Lakedaimonian armies
which the sources show masks an increase of non-'equal' Spartans, and
means only a dwindling of the privileged Spartiates. There is no proof;
one can only record an impression that this is not the answer. There
were large numbers of *neodamodeis* but their existence in separate
military units is so often recorded that we can safely assume their
absence from Spartan ranks in any significant number when they go
unmentioned. There were *hypomeiones* or people like them in the Spartan ranks and their numbers were probably increasing but I do not
believe that they were more than a sizable handful even by 371. In what
follows a Lakedaimonian army is assumed to consist of *perioikoi* and of
Spartans, and 'Spartans' means Spartiates with a smallish admixture of
the underprivileged.

First then the army organisation through which the population can
best be measured. At Plataia 5,000 Spartans, on what was probably a
thirty-five-year call-up, served with 5,000 *perioikoi* and there was a
unit, of unknown size, called a *lochos* drawn from the obe of Pitana,
presumably therefore a Spartan unit. After 371 the army consisted of
twelve units called *lochoi*; they are described as 'citizen' units but almost
certainly included *perioikoi*. For the period between, both Xenophon
and Thucydides describe an army of six units (though they give them
different names, *mora* and *lochos*) and neither explicitly includes or ex-
cludes *perioikoi* from the muster. The evidence is:

1. In 425 the Spartans put 420 men on to the island of Sphakteria,
drawn by lot from 'all the *lochoi*'. Those who surrendered were 120
Spartans and about 170 non-Spartans, i.e. *perioikoi*.

2. Thucydides numbers the army at Mantinea in 418. His figure for
the six *lochoi* on a thirty-two-year call-up is 3,072 (a *lochos* of 512, made
up of four *pentekostyes* each containing four *enomotiai*), but this is substantially fewer than we need to make sense of the battle.

3. The *mora* is first mentioned by Xenophon in 403 and in 390 the
strength of one *mora* is given as 'about 600'. From the context this
seems to be an exaggeration, but is likely to be about the normal

strength since other sources for other occasions give 500 (Ephoros), 700 (Kallisthenes) and 900 (Polybios), the last probably speaking of a different period.

4. At Nemea in 394 the army was some 6,000 strong.

5. In his *Lakedaimonion Politeia* Xenophon describes an army of six *morai*, each containing four *lochoi* composed of two *pentekostyes* which in turn were made up of two *enomotiai*, i.e. with sixteen *enomotiai* in each *mora*.

6. At Leuktra four out of the six *morai* were engaged, the call-up being thirty-five years, but no numbers are given except that according to Xenophon only 700 of those present were Spartiates.

Now 700 men could not make up 4 *morai* and it is therefore often assumed that something over 1,500 *perioikoi* must have served with them and that this intermingling went back as far as Mantinea and Pylos. Thucydides will be using the word *lochos* to describe a *mora* and will have missed out one whole level in his calculations, the real *lochos* of which there will have been two to each *mora*. The number of Lakedaimonians at Mantinea is thus increased to over 6,000, giving roughly 1,000 to each *mora*. Xenophon too, or his text, must be wrong in the number of units he gives to the *mora* in the *Lak. Pol.* for the revised Thucydides has thirty-two not sixteen *enomotiai* to the *mora* (there are of course the other disagreements on the relative sizes of the various units).

The story then is that at some time after 479, perhaps around 465 when the earthquake might call for changes, a system in which Spartans and *perioikoi* served in separate units was abandoned and the *morai*, in which *perioikoi* were included, were introduced; the proportion of *perioikoi* then continued to increase as Spartan numbers dwindled, and applying the proportions of the Pylos prisoners to the revised Thucydidean total for Mantinea we may guess that it included about 2,500 Spartans and about 3,500 *perioikoi*. The Spartans themselves were now redistributed—such things as the *lochos* of Pitana had vanished, for in 390, Xenophon records, there were men from the *oba* of Amyklai serving in more than one *mora* and men in one *mora* had close relatives in another.

But it is hard to believe that Thucydides and Xenophon should both make the same mistake about the size of the largest unit (16 *enomotiai* of 30–35 men) whatever name they give it, *lochos* or *mora*; even harder to believe that Thucydides, after all the pains he took, should have missed out one whole level at Mantinea and should not have realised that this produced too small a total. Moreover the *mora* of a thousand or more which the theory demands is substantially higher than any figure given by other sources.

Finally there can be no doubt that Xenophon in the *Lak. Pol.* believes that he is writing about a purely Spartan army, not an army contaminated with *perioikoi*. Indeed why contaminate? The *agoge* was designed to produce not just a skilful hoplite but a skilful phalanx. Surely its efficiency would be damaged by the admixture of comparatively amateur *perioikoi*, surely better to have one highly competent section of the line and another less competent—at least until the competent section shrank to a size at which its competence was no longer significant.

I therefore suggest, with much hesitation, an alternative solution; that in the army of Mantinea *perioikoi* and Spartans still fought apart, that Thucydides has given the numbers and the units of the Spartans alone, ignoring the *perioikoi*, and that Xenophon (or his text) is simply wrong in the number of Spartans he gives for Leuktra. Thucydides has still been grossly misleading but his error becomes, to my mind, less frightening. To tamper with Xenophon's text is rash, but as we shall see there is another reason for doubting it.

In all this confusion there is some firm ground. There was a change in the organisation of the army somewhere between the united Pitanatans of 479 and the dispersed Amyklaians of 390. There was a shortage of manpower already acutely felt in the Archidamian War— the anxiety for the few prisoners of Pylos is one sign, even more striking is the appearance of *neodamodeis* as a regular feature in the military system for a state like Sparta does not arm, train and in some sense liberate its slaves without pressing reason. But doubts about the organisational change make it impossible to measure, and therefore properly to explain the shortage. In one line the Spartan field army of 5,000 of 479 has become 2,500 by 418 and 1,050 by 371 (the 700 of Leuktra plus 350 left at home); on the other the 5,000 have become 3,360 by 418 and the number for 371 is unknown—an easy emendation would produce 1,700 for Leuktra, i.e. 2,550 for the active army. There are two further bits of evidence; Aristotle claims that at some point before he was writing (he may mean about the time of Leuktra) the Spartans numbered less than a thousand; Plutarch that there were still 700 Spartiates about 250 B.C.

On either line (5,000/2,500/1,050 or 5,000/3,360/2,550) the decline would be fairly steady from 479 till 371. But then, if Xenophon is right about Leuktra, it would have to be checked thereafter; if he is wrong it would have accelerated slightly to bring numbers down to Plutarch's 700 in 250. If Aristotle is thinking of the time of Leuktra, he more or less confirms Xenophon's text; if of the years that followed, he could be reflecting a sudden and dramatic drop in the 360's, the combined result of casualties in the battle (400 Spartans were killed) and the economic disaster that followed with the loss of Messenia. It need hardly be said that on *a priori* grounds the second view is preferable.

But one thing is clear, the decline did begin well before 371, even well before Mantinea, and was continuous. We must therefore look not for some sudden disaster (e.g. the earthquake of 465) to explain it but for a long-standing condition of society—in a healthy community losses, even serious losses from earthquakes, epidemics or defeats, are soon restored. In this instance the only single disaster which could have long-term effects, the loss of Messenia, comes too late to explain anything but the quickening of a process already well established.

Aristotle saw the answer in a feature of the Spartan laws of inheritance. At Athens an heiress had to marry her male next-of-kin, so preserving property inside the family, in Sparta she could be disposed of by father or guardian as he chose, naturally therefore towards existing wealth. Such a practice could indeed be disastrous given three further and more fundamental conditions: that the official allotment of land to the individual, his public *kleros*, was inadequate; that there was no source of new blood; and that there was a general unwillingness to produce children. All three were present, though all three have their problems.

(a) The *kleros*. There were two traditions about land-tenure in Sparta, (i) that all Spartans had an equal inalienable lot, (ii) that there were gross inequalities in landed wealth. Aristotle provides the solution when he distinguishes between an inalienable 'ancient share' and some other alienable type, one would guess between the public allotment and the private holding. Only Plutarch states the mechanics of allotments, a *kleros* to each child at birth, presumably reverting to the state at death; there is no knowing the reliability of his source. No one tells us where in Laconia or Messenia the public land was to be found, nor how good it was, nor how large the allotment was. Large enough to support the Spartan, his family and the helots who worked it, and to provide the required contribution to the *sussition*; but probably not much larger, for what else was needed in the seventh century? But however much Spartans may have tried to ignore the outside world in the centuries that followed, they cannot have failed gradually to raise their standards as their neighbours, even their own *perioikoi*, began to take advantage of the new economic life, much more so when their own contact with the rest of Greece increased in the fifth and fourth centuries—the greed and easy corruptibility of Spartans abroad was notorious. But the *kleros* could not support extra luxury, even of the modest kind that domestic fashion might allow; private property would become essential. In other words it is possible that by Aristotle's day the *kleros* had become irrelevant to a Spartan's survival as a Spartan.

(b) New blood. Among the mysterious words that occur describing peculiar groups at Sparta is one, *mothakes*. These are the only recorded source of reinforcement for the Spartans. They were men of uncertain, even perhaps sometimes of helot, origin, who were nevertheless attached to young Spartans in the *agoge* which they shared with them, and there is a hint that if they were outstanding enough they could be made full Spartans (in one story Lysander is said to have been a *mothax*; so is Gylippos whose father Kleandridas had lost his citizenship in 446 when Gylippos will have been a boy). But promotion to the privileged circle for a *mothax* was probably much rarer than demotion as a *hypomeion*. Aristotle reports a claim that in early days Sparta was open to recruitment from outside; it may be true or false. But we must certainly believe that in his own day the road was virtually closed.

(c) The birth-rate. The prospect of an almost automatic grant of a *kleros* can have done nothing to discourage the production of more little Spartans, so long as the *kleros* was adequate. But as soon as it became inadequate, the Spartan family found itself faced with the problem of every closed aristocracy—how to preserve its economic advantage, how not to dissipate its wealth by creating too many new bodies to share it—and like so many others it simply ceased to reproduce itself. There were counter-measures—the father of three sons was excused from some, perhaps all, military duty; but which is better, to miss a battle or two, or to know that an estate will remain intact?

And with a falling birth-rate and increasing demands on a completely static economy, the only answer for the many who found themselves with a daughter rather than a son was to find for her, and the land that she took with her, the richest home that could be found, or could be bought by a rich dowry, again in land.

The right of free disposal of property by gift or will is said by Plutarch, perhaps following Phylarchos, to have been established by a law which he conceives as belonging to the fourth century, the work of a certain Epitadeus. Aristotle knew nothing of this near contemporary figure and states it as a Lykourgan regulation. As we have seen the roots of the trouble it is said to have produced lie well behind the fourth century; Epitadeus, if he existed, does not belong to the fourth century or, if he does, did not create the trouble; nor did anything else of the same period. The loss of Messenia broke Sparta, and, whether or not many of the *kleroi* were in Messenia, the loss must have given many individual Spartans as well as the Spartan state a terrible blow. But it broke Sparta because Sparta was already fragile, and she was fragile for one reason only—there is no such thing as a caste of 'Equals' which can maintain itself when 'Equality' becomes something from which outsiders are excluded rather than something to which they can aspire.

BIBLIOGRAPHY

On the army and the population apart from Michell and Chrimes (General Bibliography) A. J. Toynbee *JHS 33* (1913) 249 ff.; H. T. Wade-Gery, *CQ 38* (1944) (*Essays* 71 ff.); on inheritance, D. Asheri, *Historia 12* (1963) 1 ff.; on the birth-rate, K. J. Dover, *Bull. Inst. Class. Stud.* (1964).

14

SPARTA IN DEFEAT

In the crisis of 370, with a Theban army facing them across the Eurotas, the Spartans armed 6,000 helots and promised them their freedom if they fought well. The courage which they showed in their still confidently unwalled city was typical; so was the fact that, according to Xenophon, 'they feared the number of the helots when they saw them ranged alongside them and thought that they were too many'. The aged Agesilaos who took command again in the crisis showed as much courage and as much conservatism. There is no sign in the next decades, or in the next century, that Sparta had understood her real position; rather the mixture as before, brutality where brutality would work, cunning of a sort and bravery, all against the old background of an unshakable assumption of superiority, of the right to rule. The horizons were now as limited as they had been in the eighth century, but the arrogant stupidity was the same.

Defence was the immediate problem. Theban armies continued to appear in the Peloponnese and in 362 one of them again reached Laconia, but the freeing of the Peloponnesian cities from Sparta's rule did not happen altogether smoothly and there could be hope that squabbles among them might open the way for a renewal of Spartan influence in some; besides there was a ready friend in Athens to whom Thebes in turn seemed a menace. Hence forays into Arkadia (one highly successful), hence by 362 a new coalition of Sparta, Athens and those Peloponnesians who had already fallen out with Thebes or the Arkadian League, that is Elis, Achaia and Arkadian Mantinea;

against them the Thebans, the Argives, the Messenians and other
Arkadians. The armies of the two alliances met in the plain between
Tegea and Mantinea and again the Thebans won. But in winning they
lost their leader, Epaminondas, and with him their power and interest
in the Peloponnese. What could have been the end for Sparta became
instead a chance for all Greeks to sit back and work out a new common
peace, for the first time without Persia or any overpowerful Greek
state to dictate it.

A rational Spartan would have welcomed the chance. A foreign army
had twice appeared in the outskirts of Sparta; now the immediate
danger was removed and the safety of Laconia could be guaranteed.
Messenia was lost for good for, even if the Spartans themselves were to
become strong enough to expand again, the Arkadians to the north
were not likely to imitate their disorganised eighth-century ancestors
in accepting the expansion, particularly now that they had established a
new city, Megalopolis, in the plain that linked Laconia with Messenia
(above p. 74). Finally, decisively, Greece was impoverished by almost
continuous war and Sparta, without Messenia, with her own outdated
economy, was poorer than most—she simply could not afford to play
at aggressive international politics. Nevertheless, when the rest of
Greece did reach agreement on the terms of a general peace after Mantinea, Sparta refused to join simply because Messenia was to be guaranteed by the treaty. And she persisted in the folly. A few years later (in
353) she was proposing an amendment to the treaty of 362 that would
satisfy the local territorial ambitions of several states—and incidentally
open her way into Messenia. Less subtly she attacked Megalopolis,
with some success. But the hard fact is that Messenia (and Megalopolis
too) stayed independent.

Her wider ambitions were there as well, ready to be fired by any
passing chance. When Philip of Macedon took over Greece after
Chaironeia in 338 he marched through the Peloponnese and, like the
Thebans thirty years before, through Laconia. This time the Spartans
did not resist, but alone among the cities they did not welcome him,
indeed they refused him entry to Sparta. Unlike the Thebans Philip
did not insist—Sparta was not worth the trouble—and when a new
Greek League was formed in 337, the League of Korinth under Macedonian control, Sparta was the only absentee. No doubt the Spartans
were proud of their 'achievement', a solitary stand against Macedon, at

any rate they were quick to take Persian aid when Alexander invaded Asia and, under Agesilaos' grandson Agis, raise an anti-Macedonian revolt in the Peloponnese in 331, its first objective, naturally, Megalopolis. The Spartan army was defeated, Agis was killed and Sparta, perforce, joined the League.

In the apparently patternless quarrelling of Alexander's successors Sparta played no great recorded part but her reappearance is true to form. In 280 Macedon, already sapped by dynastic mayhem, was overrun by a Celtic invasion from the north. A Peloponnesian might be forgiven for thinking that the Peloponnese could be united again, even under Sparta. Areus, the first significant Agiad since Pleistoanax or even Leonidas, assumed that it could be and, with less than complete backing from the Peloponnese, led an army into central Greece. Neither the expedition nor the alliance lasted long ('many states refused [to carry on], believing that the Spartans were seeking domination for themselves not freedom for the Greeks'—Justin) but Areus' ambitions did. Having survived a major invasion from the north prompted by an exiled uncle and led by Pyrrhos of Epiros (in 272) Areus began to form a new coalition, a more plausible coalition in Hellenistic terms. Rivalry in the Aegean between the Ptolemies in Egypt and Antigonos of Macedon made the Peloponnese an obvious area for Ptolemaic troublemaking, if only to divert Antigonos' attention from more important things, and Areus was quite ready to play the part of puppet-hegemon (he would not have recognised the puppet element). An alliance was formed between Athens, Sparta, Elis, Achaia and some east Arkadian cities 'against those who were enslaving the Greek cities' and in 265 the so-called Chremonidean War began with an allied attempt to relieve Athens from a Macedonian attack. The attempt failed and Areus was killed during the retreat.

In all this Sparta could not possibly succeed. The powers of the Hellenistic world were great powers and Sparta was not—in 260 the Spartan army was heavily defeated and Areus' son Akrotatos was killed by the Megalopolitans alone (the Spartans were the aggressors). She lacked the power to be great and she lacked the money to play effectively even in the second division. In 431 when Sparta still had an adequate unpaid citizen army, King Archidamos had made much of the cost of war and of Sparta's lack of state funds; in the fourth and third centuries when mercenaries had become an almost necessary part of warfare, poverty spelled failure—or a policy of peace.

To mend the poverty Spartans from time to time would use the mercenary market to their advantage and even Spartan kings appear in foreign service. Agesilaos died in 360 returning from two years as a mercenary captain in Egypt with 230 talents for the Spartan treasury; Archidamos, Agesilaos' son, was killed in 338 while serving in Italy; Leonidas II had served with Seleukos before he became king about 251; and there were others (these mercenary adventures of the royal house are sometimes seen as ignominious, but there is something sympathetic in the picture of a Spartan king earning his livelihood—and how else was he capable of earning it?). At a lower level too Spartans sought military service abroad. Cape Tainaron (its dead grey rocks are fit for nothing better) became an international mercenary centre, among other things because a good source of recruits was near at hand.

But such activity was no great help, indeed it was far more an escape for needy Spartans than an aid to a needy Sparta. Nothing could alter the fact that Laconia had an almost exclusively agricultural economy and consisted of a certain number of cultivable acres. Sparta's status in world affairs was fixed.

That is not to say that she stayed wholly immune to outside influences. Her separation from the mainstream of Greek development was always real enough, but it could never be complete, and third-century society, which has been called the most open that Greece ever knew, does seem to have influenced Sparta more noticeably than those of earlier centuries.

The much-talked-of betrayal of 'Lykourgan' values which was to call for drastic treatment later in the third century was in large part a myth. Nevertheless in several ways austerity, simplicity, modesty—in non-'Lykourgan' terms, Spartan eccentricity—were on the wane. More for example is heard of intellectual contacts; the historian Phylarchos must have visited Sparta to collect both his admiration for King Kleomenes III and much of the colourful detail with which he surrounds his story of him; the same Kleomenes had the company and the advice of the philosopher Sphairos; more surprisingly one Laconian, possibly a Spartan, Sosibios, took to antiquarian studies and wrote widely thereon. At a more mundane level, at the very end of the fourth century Sparta at last surrounded its four central villages and its akropolis with a wall. This for obvious reasons. A little later, around

280, again about 300 years behind the rest of Greece, she introduced the first Spartan coinage. Hitherto she had relied on primitive iron spits for domestic exchange, augmented for more sophisticated operations by foreign coins; now she accepted the modern world, and incidentally advertised her king's pretensions in that world—the coins carried the head of Areus surmounted by a diadem.

Areus indeed is the most striking example of the adoption of general Hellenistic ways. There had been autocratic kings in Sparta before, but, so far as we know, they had better manners or had better manners forced on them. When Pausanias the regent had tried to advertise his personal achievement at Plataia (p. 103), the Spartans at once erased the advertisement even though Plataia was quite an achievement; now the Athenian decree which marked the new alliance for the Chremonidean War could openly use the formula 'King Areus and the Lakedaimonians', an order of precedence which the coinage had already established. There is a story, often doubted, of diplomatic contact between the Spartans and the Jews in Areus' reign. Politically such a rapprochement is likely enough (the Jews were with Ptolemy at the time) but a stronger argument for the truth of the tale is the opening of the letter quoted in First Maccabees, 'Areus, King of the Spartans to . . .'.

But Areus was not alone. When he was chosen as King his uncle, Kleonymos, who thought he had a better claim, went off to mercenary service in Italy, later seized Kerkyra, and like any other Hellenistic princeling signed on with the power most likely to help him to higher things—hence Pyrrhos' invasion of the Peloponnese in 273, a rare imitation by a Spartan exile of the common Greek attempt to return to power behind foreign arms. The *possédants* who resisted the reformers of the next chapter were no less a typical Hellenistic phenomenon.

BIBLIOGRAPHY

No connected account of Spartan history is possible for this period. The general political background has been effectively described by Ed. Will, *Hist. Politique du Monde Hellenistique* (1966) with full references to date. The ancient sources, Polybios, Diodoros, Plutarch and Pausanias, offer only random insights (for the enthusiast F. W. Walbank's *Commentary* on Polybios I–VI (1957) is an excellent guide).

15

THE SECOND REVOLUTION

By far the most significant effect on Sparta of the Hellenistic world was the appearance of these *possédants* and the reaction to them. For the second time in her history Sparta was on the verge of political greatness—and for the second time she failed. The second attempt was no less honourable than the first; it was unfortunately rather less successful.

The economic history of mainland Greece in the century after Alexander is far from clear. Very crudely, his conquests brought immediate wealth, in booty if nothing else, enormous opportunities in the exploitation of the new eastern territories, and a great challenge for the homeland in maintaining itself against the new greater Greek world. To the opportunities Greece reacted as in the eighth century she had reacted to the comparable opportunities of colonisation, superbly in that they were taken at once. But the new wealth created new, eighth-century-type, problems—the poor became poorer and the rich richer, or rather there was a shake-up of wealth which in the mainland produced a poorer poor and a richer rich, this because the mainland could not face the challenge of the new provinces. The middle-class (in ancient terms the small shopkeeper, manufacturer or farmer) was crushed and the cushion between the extremes of wealth and poverty was removed.

In Sparta the process was different; it had to be because the economic background was so strange. It is likely enough that Laconia felt the competition of Alexandria, Rhodes and the rest rather less than, say, Athens, but in so far as such things were felt, they were even more disastrous. Elsewhere a man at the borderline could fight, but in Sparta, given the survival of the social rules, there was a fixed point at which he simply ceased to count.

At the same time there was in the Lykourgan tradition a clear invitation to revolution such as no other Greek state had. All Spartans had been created 'equal' but now 100 were very rich, 700 existed as full citizens and perhaps 2,000 had been demoted recently enough to remember what equality had been. Nothing prompts a revolution so quickly as a definition and it is therefore no surprise that Sparta led the third-century poor in revolt. The pity is that a combination of Spartan conservatism and accidental Roman intervention killed the general revolt they might have led.

The career of the two kings who first tried to tackle the problem, Agis IV and Kleomenes III, is described by Plutarch in great and approving detail. Two gallant young reformers are cut off, like the Gracchi in Rome, before they can do the good they wished to do. Plutarch's source for their lives was Phylarchos who was firmly biassed in favour of Kleomenes, and was himself not without the moralising tendencies which Plutarch brings out so passionately. It is a bad beginning for the construction of a true story—the only encouragement being that the few scraps of non-Phylarchean evidence which survive suggest that much of the fact was not in dispute, only the interpretation.

Modern historians of the late nineteenth and twentieth century were quick to see in Agis and Kleomenes, as they saw in the Gracchi, radical reformers of good nineteenth- or twentieth-century stamp and words like 'socialism' crept into the argument, but just as the Gracchi have tended to lose their ideals in more recent studies and to appear as traditional operators of the Roman political machine, so the Spartan pair have become 'traditional Spartan patriots'. Of course Agis and Kleomenes were not 'socialists'—there was no Greek word for 'socialism'— but it is equally wrong to suggest that they had no social programme. The unanswerable question is whether this programme was devised by them for the greater good of the world at large, of Spartans, of Sparta, or of themselves.

The essential point is that they had a programme, that it appealed to a majority of Spartans and that it might have appealed to a majority in Greece, given the luck which they lacked from the start.

Agis IV came to the Eurypontid throne in 244, and quickly drew up his proposals for change, a cancellation of debts, a complete redistribution of land throughout Laconia to produce 4,500 citizens and 15,000 perioikic lots (it would seem that by now Sparta was taking a more direct hand in controlling the perioikic communities), and the reintroduction of strict Lykourgan training for the citizens whose numbers were to be made up from the existing 700 and the 2,000 or so *hypomeiones* together with selected *perioikoi* and foreigners. The debt-proposals won warm support, some of it even among the rich (the largest land-owner can still be in debt), but redistribution made its strongest appeal to the landless or near-landless *hypomeiones* who were voteless. A few of the rich gave Agis their unselfish backing but most were bitterly hostile, among them the elderly Agiad king, Leonidas II; even the poorer citizens, we may imagine, were divided.

The split was Agis' undoing. One rich supporter, Lysander by name, became ephor for 243 and introduced the proposals to the assembly where Agis countered Leonidas' objections and won enthusiastic approval by offering his own and his family's estates for redistribution. But a little later in the *Gerousia* he failed, just failed, to win a majority for proceeding (see p. 48). Lysander then invoked ephors' ancient rights and had Leonidas deposed but when his own year of office expired his successors turned out to be hostile to Agis' plans (a hint that opinion among those who elected them was not solidly behind reform) and they too had to be deposed, by Agis, on the grounds that ephors were powerless when the kings agreed—a compliant Agiad, Kleombrotos II, had been appointed in Leonidas' place. So far so good, but suddenly Agis decided on a compromise, persuaded to it by his uncle, Agesilaos, hitherto his supporter and now a suffect ephor. The cancellation of debts was to go through (Agesilaos, it was said, was heavily in debt), the redistribution of land was to be delayed (Agesilaos was a large landowner). It is hard to see why Agis should have agreed. Loss of nerve, inexperience, whatever the reason, it was a sad mistake. Those who now had what they wanted were prepared to sit back, those who wanted more were disheartened, and when Agis lost still more credit in an abortive military expedition to the Isthmos (see below) while Agesilaos behaved more and more as master of Sparta (he proposed to extend his ephorate for a second year), the active opponents of change were able to bring about Leonidas' return from exile and a summary trial and execution for Agis (in 241).

In the middle of the third century the pattern of Peloponnesian politics was changed by the development of the Achaian League, an association which by the time of Agis included Achaia proper and much of Arkadia together with Korinth, Sikyon and Argos; at its head was an able, though not very likable schemer, Aratos. Like the Spartans, Aratos had vague Ptolemaic support against the Macedonians and was thoroughly hostile to the Aitolian federation which, with or without Macedonian help, was always ready to encroach from the north. It was against an Aitolian invasion that Agis was summoned by Aratos in 242 to a joint defence of the Peloponnese, so pointlessly that one almost suspects collusion between the right-wing Aratos and Agis' right-wing opponents at home.

Be that as it may, the man who took on Agis' part as a reformer of Sparta saw Aratos and his Achaians as the first enemy. Kleomenes III was a son of Leonidas and had been married by him to Agis' widow— good land of which she had plenty should not be wasted. But the girl who brought rich estates to the marriage also brought Agis' ideas and she inspired her husband with them. So, with rather more political talent than Agis, Kleomenes began the second and much more serious round of revolution. In a series of quick and audacious campaigns he established himself as Aratos' equal or superior in the field and then, without Agis' squeamishness, in 227, staged a sudden coup in Sparta in which four ephors died and eighty opponents were exiled. He then abolished the ephorate on the grounds that in origin the office had been created by the kings to assist the kings, and therefore presumably could be dispensed with when it failed to assist—there is a hint of the same theory on the ephorate behind Agis' deposition of the hostile board (cf. above p. 145). Agis' brother Archidamos who had fled to Messenia in 241 was summoned back to the Eurypontid throne but was at once assassinated by Agis' old enemies, some thought with Kleomenes' approval. In his place Kleomenes made his own brother, Eukleidas, king. The powers and probably the composition of the *Gerousia* may have been altered and a new magistracy, the *patronomoi*, created to take over at least some of its judicial functions. Finally the land was at last redistributed into 4,000 lots, and *perioikoi* as well as *hypomeiones* were recruited to occupy them while Lykourgan training and Lykourgan habits were re-imposed under the guidance of Kleomenes' philosopher friend Sphairos.

Domestically all this was a great success. Much was being done in Lykourgos' name that would have astonished him, but the problems that faced third-century Sparta, poverty and inequality, were basically the same as those that he had solved, the solution was basically the same and so, apparently, was the result, a popular *eunomia*. But the over-confident 'equals' of the seventh century had marched out to disaster at Hysiai; those of 227 made the same mistake, led on no doubt by the old ambition for hegemony, in part very probably by the old arrogance which did not stop to count the opposition, but in part by something which was probably new, the desire to carry their *eunomia* abroad to other Greeks who were as much in need of it.

Certainly the expectation of general reform was one of the reasons for Kleomenes' remarkable military successes during the next year or so. Most of eastern Arkadia, even Argos and much of the Argolid, fell to him and for a moment it seemed as if the Achaian League as a whole would accept Spartan leadership. But a united Peloponnese under a leader like Kleomenes would have come near to being a power in the Hellenistic world, particularly if it had begun to broadcast its appeal to the poor wherever they were, a threat to the delicate balance between the other powers which could not be ignored. So while Ptolemy stood aside and in the end even stopped the small subsidies which he had been paying to Kleomenes, Antigonos Doson from Macedon took a hand.

Much has been made by ancient and modern historians of the 'great betrayal' which allowed Antigonos to intervene. Aratos who had won freedom for the Peloponnese by expelling the Macedonians from Korinth in 243 now himself appealed to Antigonos and offered to restore Korinth to him. It was a fairly sordid deal and certainly the turning-point of the war, but probably more dramatic than decisive for Antigonos would surely have found another opening and chances are that he would have won in the end, much as he did.

Not that the Macedonian victory was easy. In 224 Antigonos recovered Argos, in 223 several Arkadian cities, but in return Kleomenes captured and destroyed Megalopolis. Then to reinforce his treasury and his army he sold freedom to some 6,000 helots and hired more mercenaries with the cash. As a result he faced the last campaign of 222 with an army of 10,000; Antigonos had 30,000. They met at Sellasia, to the north of Sparta on the road to Tegea, and there Kleomenes chose his position well and fought a long, skilful and courageous battle. But in the end the Spartans were overwhelmed and Kleomenes fled, to Sparta and thence to Egypt. Sparta was in Macedon's hands.

All are agreed that Antigonos showed magnanimity, but there is very little evidence on how he showed it. Sparta was enrolled in a Hellenic League which Antigonos had created and a Macedonian governor was installed; she lost to Messenia such land as she still held across Taygetos, Dentheliatis, Teleklos' old acquisition in the Nedon valley; otherwise 'Antigonos restored the ancestral constitution'. Polybios, who uses these words, probably meant no more than that a constitution of some kind was restored, for to him Kleomenes, having abolished the ephorate and the Eurypontid kingship, had become a tyrant and in his language almost anything other than tyranny was an 'ancestral constitution'. The details then can only be inferred or guessed. No attempt was made to fill the vacant kingship or to replace Kleomenes, but the ephorate was re-established. On the other hand the *patronomoi*, if Kleomones did indeed create them, were allowed to survive for they figure in Sparta's later history. The terrible losses at Sellasia (Plutarch, implausibly, says that only 200 Spartans survived) must have made nonsense of the new land pattern but how the problem was resolved is not known; nor is anything heard of Sphairos' pride, the rejuvenated *agoge*.

By and large, however, it is likely that power moved back into the old hands, though not for long, and never unchallenged. In the course of the next fifteen years kings, Agiad and Eurypontid, were created (after Kleomenes' death in Egypt in 219), deposed, exiled, recalled; two boards of ephors were massacred; revolutions were proclaimed or suspected; in all the confusion no clue to the background except that it was full of bitterness and the old unrest. But in 206 the third great revolutionary appeared.

The Eurypontid 'king', of very doubtful right, was a minor. His guardian, Machanidas, was killed in battle against the Achaians in 206 and a new regent took his place, Nabis, son of Demaratos, descended from the Demaratos who had fled to Persia in 490. For Nabis there is no friendly source like Phylarchos; nearly all our information comes directly or indirectly through Livy from Polybios for whom Nabis was an even fouler tyrant than Kleomenes. And foul indeed his crimes appear—the murder of his ward, general persecution, assassination, execution, cruelty, treachery through fourteen years while he peopled

Sparta with a gang of mercenary brigands and Laconia's coasts with pirates. The facts are probably correct, Nabis was certainly far tougher, far more ruthless than Agis or even Kleomenes, but there is no reason to think that his aims were very different or less sincere.

The sources have only casual allusions to his social measures. He confiscated the estates of his wealthy opponents and redistributed them to the needy, including some of his mercenaries (this could have been part of a general redistribution of land but nothing is said of it). He set free many slaves (helots are not specifically mentioned but may be intended). And these moves, perhaps with others we hear nothing of (abolition of debts, for example), were enough to give him the eager support of an army some 10,000 strong.

But, as Kleomenes discovered, 10,000 was not enough to stand against a major power and Nabis, like Kleomenes, had to face a major power—though he did rather less to provoke the trouble. After Antigonos' occupation, Sparta had soon reverted to a more natural anti-Achaian foreign policy and by 206 she found herself ranged with Rome and others against Macedon and Achaia in Rome's first anti-Macedonian campaigns. But during Rome's second and major intervention in Greece (from 200) the Achaians abandoned Macedon for the Roman side and at the same time the Romans became more and more identified with the oligarchs of Greece. Philip V of Macedon on the other hand began to look to would-be democratic revolutionaries for his support. So Nabis was drawn both by ideology and a hatred for Achaia towards the Macedonian camp and although he cleverly avoided making any overt move he did accept one gift from Philip, the possession of Argos when Philip could no longer hold it. Nor was his public help to the Romans more energetic than it need be.

Thus when the Roman commander, Flamininus, and his advisers came to settle Greek affairs after the defeat of Philip, ideology again (Nabis had extended his social reforms to Argos) and suspicion of his loyalty, together perhaps with a genuine dislike of the piracy and brigandage which he certainly encouraged, dictated punishment. Flamininus invaded Laconia, occupied much of it and, brushing aside Nabis' quite correct claim that he had done nothing to break his earlier alliance with Rome, laid siege to Sparta. A meeting of the Spartan *ekklesia* (so much for the claim that Nabis was a 'tyrant' pure and simple) refused to consider the terms which Flamininus offered though

Nabis was ready to accept them—he saw that resistance was unreal and that Rome would not be too severe on a useful counterpoise to the ambitions of the Achaians—but a few days' fighting changed the *ekklesia*'s mind. A truce was accepted by which Sparta lost Argos, her perioikic cities on the coast (for the first time), her fleet and other things; in exchange Nabis and his system were to survive in Sparta.

It was now that he made, or may have made (the story as Livy tells it hardly makes sense), his first mistake. The Aitolian League which had also suffered Roman displeasure began to plan a revolt, relying on intervention from the one remaining great Hellenistic power, Antiochos in Syria. Locally they approached Philip in Macedon and Nabis who at once responded, Livy says, by trying to recover the coastal cities, so provoking a just, violent and successful Achaian reprisal. Foiled, the Aitolians then sent a thousand troops, ostensibly to help Nabis, in fact to kill him and secure Sparta. So Nabis died but the Aitolians were massacred to a man by the outraged Spartans. And to bring peace all round the Achaians then moved in to add Sparta to the Achaian League.

But if Nabis had in fact succumbed to Aitolian temptation why did Flamininus try to dissuade the Achaians from their just reprisal, as Livy said he did, and why above all did the Aitolians murder a man who was their accomplice and still had, as the event showed, wholehearted support at home? Rather, I think, Nabis must have rejected Aitolian overtures but may have seen in the general crisis (and in Flamininus' goodwill?) a chance for some quiet recovery of what he thought of as Sparta's own, not reckoning with Achaian violence or with Aitolian treachery—an error still, but one that even a clever man might make.

At any rate he died, and with him the Spartan revolution. What remains inexplicable is the submission to Achaia which followed. Achaian oratory (as Livy thought) or just exhaustion? Whatever it was it was the end of Sparta's independent history.

BIBLIOGRAPHY

On the general economic background see W. W. Tarn and G. T. Griffiths, *Hellenistic Civilisation* 3rd ed. (1952) or in much greater detail M. Rostovtzeff, *Social and Economic History of the Hellenistic World* (3 vols. 1941); on Agis and Kleomenes, Plutarch's *Lives* (cf. T. W. Africa, *Phylarchus and the Spartan Revolution* (1961); A. Fuks, *CQ* 12 (1962) 118 ff.); P. Cloché, *Rev. Et. Grècques* 56 (1943) 53 ff.; M. Hadas, *Class. Weekly* 12 (1932/3) 65 ff.; A. Fuks, *Athenaeum* 40 (1962) 244 ff. and *CP* 57 (1962) 161 ff.; B. Shimron, *Historia* 13 (1964) 147 ff. and *CQ* 14 (1964) 232 ff.; F. W. Walbank in *Ehrenberg Studies*, 303 ff.; on Nabis, Shimron, *CP* 61 (1966) 1 ff.; J. Briscoe, *Past and Present* 36 (1967) 1 ff.; C. Mossé, *Cahiers d'hist.* (Lyon) 9 (1964), 313 ff.

CONCLUSION

This account of Spartan history has not shown much sympathy with Sparta; sympathy is killed by the narrow-minded jealousy she showed for so long to anyone whose power looked like becoming greater than her own and by the utter inhumanity of her behaviour when her own power was supreme.

To redress the balance a little some things can be said in her favour and they are not unimportant. Sparta was the first state we know of to accept the idea that all citizens, *qua* citizens, were equal and to devise a constitution which allowed these citizens a defined and substantial say in running their city. Their rights were much more limited, their numbers much narrower than those of the Athenians but to criticise Sparta for that is irrelevant, as it is irrelevant to complain that they failed to make citizens of helots or *perioikoi*, as irrelevant as it would be to blame Rutherford for not inventing the hydrogen bomb when he split the atom. The idea was there, it was applied remarkably effectively and was accepted by the defeated aristocracy with far less trouble than was usual for Greece or has been usual elsewhere since.

The nationalist military expansion which followed calls for no praise but it is a natural enough consequence of domestic revolution to escape much blame, and the good sense (and again the lack of quarrelling) with which it was given up in the mid-sixth century for a peaceful extension of Spartan influence in the Peloponnese and the even greater good sense with which the growth of a federal constitution among the allies was accepted again put Sparta at the head of Greek political development.

It was after the Persian Wars that the rot set in. During the next century or so Sparta did untold harm abroad and showed little sense at home. Changes were needed but, pickled in self-satisfaction, the Spartans would not move. Nevertheless there is one good feature in their obstinacy. As a leading Athenian democrat once remarked, and as recent events in Greece have underlined, there is merit in loyalty to a constitution, even to a bad one. Nor was the Spartan constitution altogether bad. Her political institutions served her quite well throughout and although Aristotle could find fault with some of them, the ephorate for example, it was in the social system that he rightly saw her chief defects. It was Sparta's failure to see the need for social mobility that destroyed her.

Nevertheless when that need became absolutely desperate not only in Sparta but throughout the whole of Greece, it was again a Spartan who took the first steps to remedy it, not an underprivileged Spartan but a king. And while there were sporadic attempts at change elsewhere it was again only in Sparta that we see a strong and persistent revolutionary movement running right through to the last collapse. A touch of the old stubbornness perhaps, but in a better cause, and with very much more than a touch of the real spirit of Lykourgos.

Roman rule restored, repaired, preserved the Lykourgan façade for tourists' pleasure; but with Achaian help it had made a more thorough job of destroying the spirit. A sad end to an unhappy but not entirely discreditable story.

GENERAL BIBLIOGRAPHY

There are the following general books on Sparta in English:

W. Den Boer, *Laconian Studies* (1954)—chronology and institutions.

K. M. T. Chrimes, *Ancient Sparta* (1949)—mainly on institutions.

G. L. Huxley, *Early Sparta* (1962)—a narrative history to 490 B.C.

A. H. M. Jones, *Sparta* (1967)—a narrative history through to the Imperial period.

H. Michell, *Sparta* (1952)—also institutional.

E. N. Tigerstedt, *The Legend of Sparta in Classical Antiquity* (1965).

Also valuable are:

F. Kiechle, *Lakonien und Sparta* (1963).

F. Ollier, *Le Mirage Spartiate*, 2 vols. (1933 and 1943).

P. Roussel, *Sparte*, 2nd ed. (1960).

Michell, Den Boer and Huxley give substantial bibliographies, the last up to 1960 for the early period. The following works, mainly more recent, may be added:

T. W. Africa, *Phylarchus and the Spartan Revolution* (1961).

A. Andrewes, 'The government of classical Sparta', *Ancient Society and Institutions (Studies presented to V. Ehrenberg)* 1 ff.

E. Badian, 'Agis III', *Hermes 95* (1967).

J. Boardman, 'Artemis Orthia and Chronology', *BSA 58* (1963) 1 ff.

G. Bockisch, 'Die Lakedaimonier auf Lesbos', *Klio 43–5* (1965) 67 ff.

P. A. Brunt, 'Spartan strategy in the Archidamian War', *The Phoenix 19* (1965) 255 ff.

D. Butler, 'Competence of the demos in the Spartan rhetra', *Historia 11* (1962) 385 ff.

B. Cardavus, 'Juden und Spartaner', *Hermes 95* (1967) 317 ff.

R. M. Cook, 'Spartan History and Archaeology', *CQ 12* (1962) 156 ff.

G. Devereux, 'La psychanalyse et l'histoire', *Annales Econom. Soc. Civ. 20* (1965) 18 ff.

P. H. Epps, 'Opinion of the Spartans since the second century B.C.', *Stud. in honour of Ullman* (1960) 35 ff.

H. J. Erasmus, 'Two notes on the early history of Sparta', *Proc. Afr. Class. Ass. 4* (1961) 3 ff.

W. G. Forrest, 'The date of the Lykourgan Reforms at Sparta', *Phoenix 17* (1963) 157 ff.; 'Legislation at Sparta', ibid. *21* (1967) 11 ff.

A. Fuks, 'Non-Phylarchean tradition of the programme of Agis IV', *CQ 12* (1962) 118 ff.; 'The Spartan citizen-body in the mid-third century B.C. and its enlargement proposed by Agis IV', *Athenaeum 40* (1962) 244 ff.; 'Agis, Cleomenes and Equality', *CP 57* (1962) 161 ff.

J. R. Grant, 'Leonidas' last stand', *The Phoenix 15* (1961) 14 ff.

P. Janni, *La Cultura di Sparta Arcaica* (1965).

L. H. Jeffery, 'The Pact of the first Settlers at Cyrene', *Historia 10* (1961) 139 ff.

A. H. M. Jones, 'The Lycurgan Rhetra' in *Ancient Society and Institutions (Studies presented to V. Ehrenberg)* 165 ff.

M. A. Levi, 'Studi Spartani i-iv' (on Dorians, tribes and *obai*, kings and helots), *RII 96* (1962) 479 ff., 500 ff., 513 ff., 523 ff.

A. Lippold, 'Pausanias von Sparta und die Perser', *Rh. Mus. 108* (1965) 320 ff.

D. Lotze, 'Lysander und d. Pelop. Krieg' (Dissertation Jena, 1962); 'Mothakes', *Historia 11* (1962) 427 ff.

R. Meister, 'Die Spartanischen Altersklassen . . .', *Sb Wien, Phil.-Hist. Klasse,* 241.5.

L. Moretti, *Richerche sulle Leghe Greche* (1962).

C. Mossé, 'Nabis, "roi" de Sparte', *Cahiers d'histoire* (Lyon) *9* (1964), 313 ff.

P. Oliva, ' "Lycurgan" Sparta', *Zhiva Antika 16* (1966) 123 ff.

J. H. Oliver, *Demokratia* (1960).

F. Paenhuysen, 'Paralleles entre les institutions de Sparte et d'Athenes', *Bull. Assoc. Budé* (1964) 342 ff.

C. Pavese, 'Un emendazione alla *retra* di Licurgo' *Rivista de Filologia 95* (1967) 129 ff.

L. Pearson, 'The Pseudo-history of Messenia and its authors', *Historia 11* (1962) 397 ff.

B. Shimron, 'The Spartan Polity after the defeat of Kleomenes III', *CQ 14* (1964) 232 ff.; 'Polybius and the reforms of Kleomenes III', *Historia 13* (1964) 147 ff.

C. G. Starr, 'The Credibility of Early Spartan History', *Historia 14* (1965) 257 ff.

H. T. Wade-Gery, 'The "Rhianos-Hypothesis" ' in *Ancient Society and Institutions (Studies presented to V. Ehrenberg)* 289 ff.

F. W. Walbank, 'The Spartan Ancestral Constitution in Polybius', *ibid.* 303 ff.

M. E. White, 'Some Agiad Dates', *JHS 84* (1964) 140 ff.

K. Wickert, 'D. Pelop. Bund von seiner entstehung bis zum ende d. Archid. Krieges' (Diss. Erlangen, 1964).

G. Zeilhofer, 'Sparta, Delphoi und d. Amphiktionen . . .' (Diss. Erlangen, 1959).

INDEX